Delicious in Dungeon

Ryoko Kui

14

MW00658754

Delicious in Dungeon

14

Contents

92. The Island

LA...
LAIOS!!
LAIOS! LAIOS!!
CARE-FUL!
YOU MUSTN'T DIE IN THAT FORM!!
GET UP!
WISH TO RETURN TO YOUR ORIG-INAL... FORM...
......
HEY.
IS THE DEMON TOTALLY GONE?
......
HEY.
LOOK BEHIND YOU. IT'S...

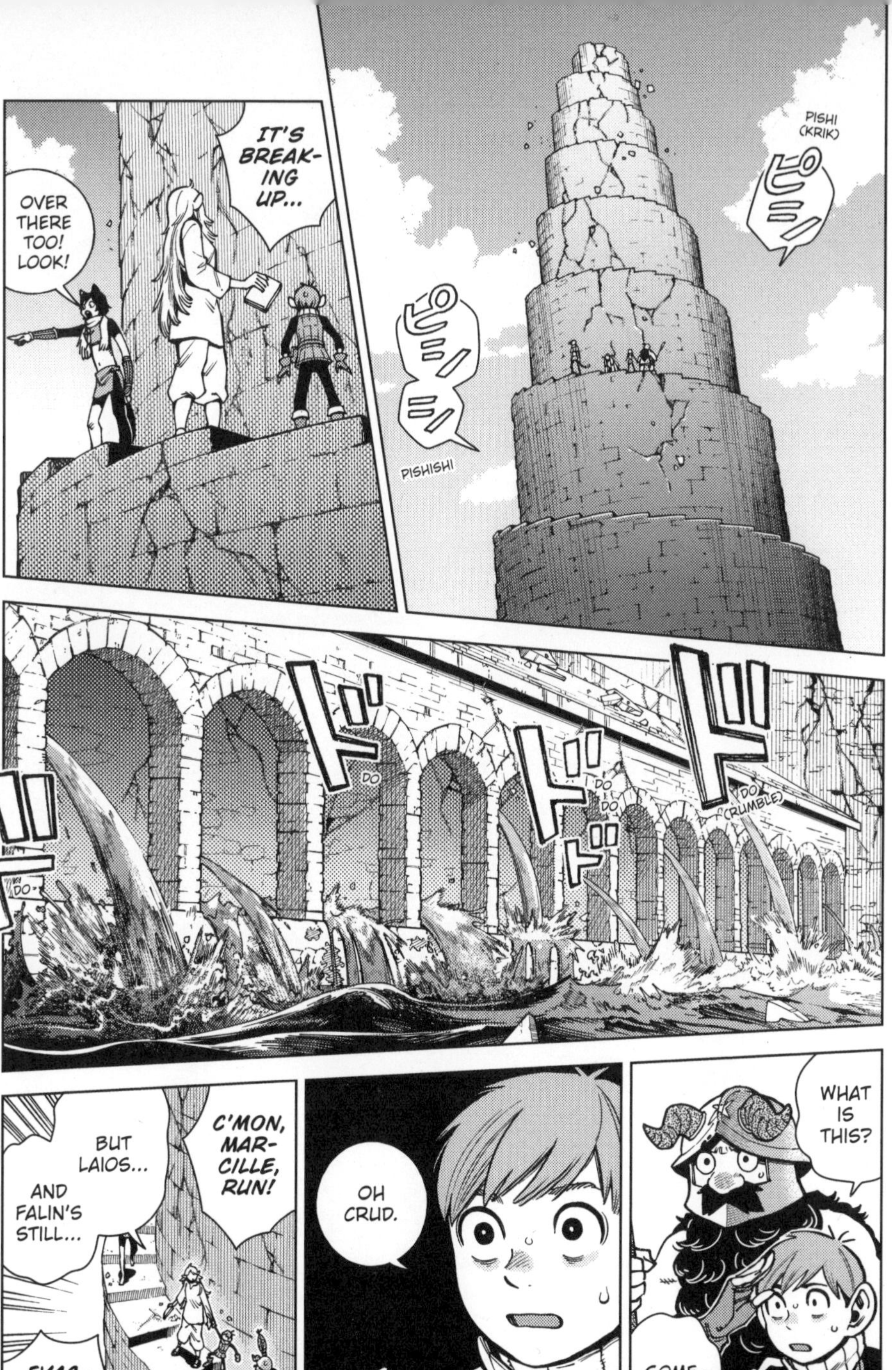
PISHI (KRIK)
PISHISHI
IT'S BREAKING UP...
OVER THERE TOO! LOOK!
DO (RUMBLE)
DO
DO
DO
DO
WHAT IS THIS?
SOMETHING'S OFF...
OH CRUD.
C'MON, MARCILLE, RUN!
BUT LAIOS...
AND FALIN'S STILL...
EVACUATING COMES FIRST!

WE HAVE TO GET TO THE SURFACE ...
THE WHOLE DUN-GEON'S COMING APART !?
IF WE DON'T MOVE FAST, IT'LL DRAG US IN!
BUT WHICH WAY IS IT!?
I THINK IT WAS...

WAIT!!
IZUTSUMI, WHAT...?
THAT WASN'T ME.
IT'S YAAD.
IT'S ME!
SISSEL TRAPPED ME IN A DOLL.
MY SOUL, I MEAN.
MY BODY SHOULD STILL BE IN HIS HOUSE.
ACTUALLY, YEAH, IT WAS.
WE USED IT AS A SHIELD.
TAKE ME THERE, PLEASE!
NOW THAT THE DUNGEON'S COLLAPSED, I'M NOT SURE HOW LONG IT WILL BE SAFE...
...BUT I CAN GUIDE YOU IF I HAVE MY BODY.
PLEASE.
FINE!

WHEEZE!
WHEEZE!
HUFF!
WATCH OUT FOR DEBRIS.
I THINK IT WAS THIS ROOM—
AUGH! MY BODY!
IT TOOK A DIRECT HIT.
WANT ME TO TRY REVIVING YOU?
NO...
THERE'S NO HOPE OF THAT.
IT DIED WHILE MY SOUL WAS GONE.
I-I'M SORRY FOR YOUR LOSS.
URGH...

...THERE'S NOTHING ELSE FOR IT.
I'LL BORROW GRAND-FATHER'S BODY!
CAN YOU DO THAT?
HE BORROWED MY FATHER'S BODY TO GO ABOVE-GROUND.
I SHOULD BE ABLE TO DO THE SAME.
IZUTSUMI, PLEASE PUT ME NEAR HIM.
SUU (BLINK)
HOW IS IT?
IT FEELS ODD, BUT...
FURA (TOTTER)
...I THINK IT WILL WORK.
I'M SORRY.
MAY I ASK ONE MORE FAVOR...?

PATA (SCAMPER)
PATA
PATA
THAT GUY...
...HAD BETTER NOT WAKE UP AND GO CRAZY ON US.
HE DOESN'T HAVE THE POWER OF THE DUNGEON LORD ANYMORE.
SISSEL DID MANY THINGS THAT WEREN'T GOOD.
HOWEVER, I'VE SEEN QUITE A BIT...
...AND I CAN'T CLAIM IT WAS ALL HIS FAULT.
I CAN'T JUST LEAVE HIM HERE ALONE.
YEAH...
ALL RIGHT. THIS WAY.
HEY! OVER HERE!

THEY'RE HERE!
THE PEOPLE OF THE GOLDEN COUNTRY.
IT'S ME. YAAD.
MASTER YAAD!?
ZAWA (MURMUR)
WHAT IN THE WORLD ...?
HM?
AGH! SISSEL !?
WHY'D YOU BRING HIM!?
HE'S STILL ALIVE !?
I'M SORRY. I'LL EXPLAIN LATER.
FOR NOW, I HAVE TO TAKE THEIR PARTY TO SAFETY.

THIS WAY!
GET ON! IT LOOKS LIKE THE WHOLE DUNGEON IS SHRINK-ING!
GO!
DO
DO (CRUMBLE)
DO
DO
DO
WHAT ABOUT THEM!?
DON'T WORRY.
EVEN IF THE PATH CRUMBLES, WE HAVE ALLIES.
DO
DO
DO
AL-LIES?
I'M SURE WE'LL MEET AGAIN.

ぼや～…
BOYA (HAZE)
TURN LEFT NEXT!
...BY "ALLIES," HE MEANT THE GHOSTS?
THINK THEY'VE FOR-GIVEN US FOR USING THEM TO MAKE SORBET?

ISN'T THIS THE ANCIENT DWARF RESER-VOIR!?
THE ORDER IS ALL SCRAM-BLED!
WATCH THE GROUND!!
WE CAN'T AFFORD TO STEP ON CHANGE-LINGS NOW!
AH! YOU'RE RIGHT.
OB-STACLE AHEAD!
WE'LL JUMP IT!
HUH!?
HUH!?
HUUH!?
AAAAH!
DO (LEAP)
DON (THUMP)
THE SECOND FLOOR!?
THE MONSTERS ARE FLEEING ALONG WITH US...

MAN-DRAKES CAN RUN!?
スタタタター〜ッ
SUTATATATAAA (SCAMPER)
I BET LAIOS WOULD HAVE LOVED THIS.
WAAAAH!
THE ARMOR'S RUNNING TOO!
OH!
THE VEG-ETABLE GOLEMS!
JIROU! SABU-ROU!
WE'RE GOING THROUGH HERE!!

THE FIRST FLOOR!!
BEGINNERS' PLAZA!!
THE SURFACE IS JUST UP THOSE STAIRS.
DISMOUNT!
AH!
BASHA (SPLASH)
THE WATER'S ALL THE WAY UP HERE.
COME, HURRY UP!
ZAAA ZAAA (FWOOSH)
IZUTSUMI. THANK YOU FOR ALL YOUR HELP.
HUH? WHY NOW?

WE'VE BEEN KEPT ALIVE BY THE DUNGEON'S POWER.
ONCE WE LEAVE, IT WON'T BE LONG BEFORE WE TURN TO DUST.
HUH?
WHAT ARE YOU TALKING ABOUT?
WHAT ABOUT JOURNEYING WITH ME TO DEFEAT THE BLACK MAGICIAN?
I'M REALLY SORRY, IZUTSUMI.
THEN—
IZUTSUMI! THERE'S NO TIME!
BE WELL.
THANK YOU.
WAIT...!
BUSHU (SPLOOSH)

DOPA (BLOOSH)
ZAZAA (FWOOOSH)
GOPOPO (BURBLE)
GOPO
GOBOBO (GURGLE)

IT'S ALL BEING WASHED AWAY...
MY DREAM.
THE ANCIENT GOLDEN CITY.
THE MONSTERS.
FALIN.
LAIOS.
......

DOBAAA (BLOOSH)
ZAZAAA (FSHHH)
NGH...
BURU (SHAKE)
BURU
KOFF! KOFF!
BA (BOLT)
YAAD!

HUH?
HUH !?
HEY. YOU'RE NOT TURNING TO DUST.
IT SEEMS NOT.
I WONDER WHY...
PTOO!
PTOO!
TO BEGIN WITH...
JYA (TRICKLE)
...THE BORDER BETWEEN THE DUNGEON AND THE SURFACE VANISHED WHEN THE WINGED LION ESCAPED.
EVEN IF THE LION'S GONE...
...IT LOOKS AS IF THE EFFECTS OF THE DUNGEON'S POWER WON'T VANISH RIGHT AWAY.
DUNGEON
DUNGEON
DUNGEON
DUNGEON
DUNGEON
DUNGEON
DUNGEON
DUNGEON
THEN WHAT WILL HAPPEN TO US?
UM...
MAYBE YOU'LL TURN TO DUST GRADU-ALLY...?
HUH!?

STILL, IN THAT CASE, I WONDER WHY THE DUNGEON COLLAPSED ...
WHOA!
?
HEY! LOOK AT THAT!
ZAAAAA (FWOOOSH)
THE ISLAND'S SPLIT IN TWO.
BUSHU (BLOOSH)
DWAH!
THERE ARE HOLES ALL OVER THE GROUND...
...AND THEY'RE SPITTING UP ALL MANNER OF THINGS FROM THE DUNGEON.
HMM...
GOBO (BLUB)
GO (BLUP)
GOPO (BURBLE)
HMM...?

GOPA
(SPLOOSH)
AAAA-AAAA-AAAH!
DO
(RUMBLE)
DO
DO
DO
DO
ZAZAAAN
(FSHHH)
MAR-CILLE!!
UGH...
NNGH...

NNH...
UHNN...
HUH?
WHAT!?
HAH...!
NA-MARI!!
YOU GUYS...
WAS THAT...
...ALL A DREAM?
HUH?
YOU'RE KID-DING...
OKAY...?
OH, THANK GOOD-NESS! YOU'RE OKAY!!

I THINK... I WAS HAVING A TERRIBLY PLEASANT DREAM...
OUT OF NOWHERE, THIS GENTLE WARMTH ENVELOPED ME...
...AND ALL MY WANTS WERE FUL-FILLED.
"OH, NOW I CAN REST EASY.
"I'LL NEVER SUFFER AGAIN," I THOUGHT, BUT THEN...
...LAIOS SHOWED UP...
...AND STARTED EATING EVERYTHING IN SIGHT.
IT GOT QUIET. THEN A VOICE SAID—
I DON'T NEED YOU ANYMORE.
FU (FFT)
—AND AS SOON AS I HEARD THAT, I GOT SPAT OUT.
PTOOO!
MAN...
WHAT A LETDOWN...
HAAAAAH...
IT WAS A NARROW ESCAPE, ALL RIGHT!?
HMM? SO...
YEAH, I GUESS IT WAS TOO GOOD TO BE TRUE...

WHAT HAPPENED TO LAIOS!?
WHAT DID THAT IDIOT DO!?
WELL...
HE FOUGHT THE DEMON AS A MON-STER...
...AND THEN YOU LOST HIM!?
HE BECAME A MONSTER IN ORDER TO DEFEAT THE DEMON!?
THAT'S INSANE...
THAT JERK!
PAN (SMACK)
I REALLY AM GONNA HAVE TO BELT HIM ONE.
BOKI (KRAK)
BOKI
SO WILL I.
THAT'LL BE A LONG LINE.

WHAT'S THAT FACE FOR, MARCILLE?
...AND FALIN'S STILL IN THE DUNGEON, FROZEN...
UUUU!
HEY, DON'T CRY.
IT'LL ALL WORK OUT.
MY DREAM WON'T COME TRUE.
THE ISLAND'S A TOTAL MESS...
I MEAN...
...LAIOS TURNED INTO A MONSTER.
GOSO (RUMMAGE)
WHAT'S UP, SHURO?
...SHH.

CHIRI (JINGLE)
チリ…
RIN (DING)
…リン…
CHIRIN
チリン…
!
THAT BELL ...!
IT'S THE TWIN OF THE ONE I GAVE LAIOS.
THIS ONE IS MADE TO RING WHEN THAT ONE DOES.
MAYBE IT'S JUST BEING SWEPT ALONG BY WATER OR WIND?
NO.
IT'S RINGING IN TIME WITH HIS FOOTSTEPS.
CHIRIN
チリン
(STEP)
CHIRIN
チリン
(STEP)
I KNOW THAT PACE ALL TOO WELL...
JIRIRIRI (JANGLE)
JIRIN
JIRIN
LET'S TRY CALLING HIM.
PITA (FREEZE)
ぴたっ…
......
......
......

THERE'S NO RESPONSE.
WHAT!?
THAT IS, EVER SINCE I GAVE THIS TO HIM...
DON'T DIE.
RIN
(JINGLE)
QUIT RUNNING.
...IT'S BEEN RINGING NONSTOP—AND IT SUDDENLY STOPPED.
DO YOU HEAR RINGING?
......
SHUT UP!
SO...
...HE'S DEFINITELY ALIVE, AND HE'S IN HIS RIGHT MIND AGAIN!!
GRAUGH!
THAT JERK...
WHAT MAKES YOU SAY THAT?
?
HE FINALLY REMEMBERED THE BELL, AND HE PANICKED.
IT'S NOT A REACTION A MONSTER WOULD HAVE.
WE'LL FIND HIM, NO MATTER WHAT.
I WON'T BE SATISFIED UNTIL I'VE PUNCHED HIM.
ME TOO.
AND ME.
MAYBE HE SENSED ALL THIS HOSTILITY...
LAIOOOS!
THAT JERK!

HEEEY!
LAIOOOS!
HEY!
COME CHECK THIS OUT.

MONSTER REMAINS?
THE SIZE IS WRONG ...
...BUT THESE ARE BITS OF THAT MONSTER.
IT'S LIKE HE JUST SHUCKED THEM OFF.
THE BELL!
チリ
CHIRI (JINGLE)
チリ
CHIRI
WHY'S HE RUNNING !?
MAYBE HE STILL LOOKS LIKE HE'S PART MONSTER?
LAIOS!
LAIOS, ARE YOU IN THERE?
LAI—

FALIN...!
WH- WHAT'S SHE DOING HERE?
KASA (RUSTLE)
KOSO (SNEAK)
GA (GRAB)
STOP!
RIGHT THIS MIN-UTE!!
HAAH...
HON-ESTLY.
EVERYONE'S WAITING FOR YOU...
...LAIOS!

SA (SHF)
WHY ARE YOU MOPING?
COME ON, GET UP.
THEY WON'T FORGIVE ME.
THEY'RE MAD, BUT NOT AS MAD AS THEY SOUND.
NO, WE'RE FURIOUS!!
OR WE WILL BE IF YOU KEEP DRAGGING YOUR FEET!
URK!
HERE, LET ME SEE YOU.
YOU DON'T STILL HAVE HORNS OR A TAIL, RIGHT?
IT WOULDN'T HAVE BEEN REWARDING TO COOK FOR YOU IN THAT FORM.
IF YOU EVER WANT YOUR HEAD CUT OFF AGAIN, LEMME KNOW.

IN ANY CASE, WE'RE GLAD YOU'RE SAFE.
HOLD YOUR HEAD HIGH AND LET THE OTHERS SEE YOU'RE WELL.
MM-HMM...
AAH!!
ドキ
DOKI (BADMP)
LAIOS!!
YOU SONUVA ...!
G'WAN, GET!
ガッ
GA (KICK)
CHAPTER 92: THE END

93. Falin -1-

ドス
DOSU (STOMP)
LAIOS!
YOU SONUVA ...!
ドス
DOSU
LOOK WHAT YOU DID!
ドス
DOSU
GHK!
I-I'M SORRY!
IT WAS ALL MY—
WELL DONE!

WASHI
WASHI (RUFFLE)
GOOD GRIEF!
WHAT A WAY TO END IT...
WHEN YOU TAKE 'EM THAT FAR, EVEN YOUR TASTES ARE PRETTY IMPRESSIVE!
SO, AFTER WHAT I DID...
...EVERY-ONE'S FINE WITH IT?
YEAH, THRILLED.
WE ARE, AT LEAST.
YOU DID WELL.
IT'S A RELIEF TO KNOW THAT I WAS A GOOD JUDGE OF CHARACTER AFTER ALL.
GET A LOAD OF YOU.
BY THE WAY...
THE WHOLE POINT OF YOUR WISH WAS TO DRIVE THE DEMON AWAY, WASN'T IT?
NEVER MIND. DON'T TELL ME.
IT WORKED. THAT'S WHAT MATTERS.

I NEVER THOUGHT WE'D BE ABLE TO LEAVE THAT COUNTRY WHILE WE LIVED.
THANK YOU. THANK YOU SO MUCH.
SAY, LAIOS.
HOW WOULD YOU LIKE TO MARRY MY LITTLE SISTER?
UM...
HOW OLD IS SHE?
SO MONSTERS WEREN'T ENOUGH, HMM? YOU ACTUALLY ATE A DEMON.
I SWEAR.
A MORE BIZARRE FOOD HAS NEVER BEEN EATEN.
WE INVITE YOU TO OUR SHIP.
WOULD YOU COME BACK TO OUR COUNTRY WITH US?
N-NOT AS A PRISONER?
DON'T GET ON THAT BOAT.

ぐっ
GU (GRIP)
THERE'LL BE NO WORK FOR ADVENTURERS NOW.
YOUR EXPERIENCES WILL BE USEFUL TO US.
WE CAN'T HAVE THAT!
HE MUST INHERIT THIS LAND, AS MY GRANDFATHER WISHED.
THIS LAND!?
THE ISLAND'S MINE!!
ISLAND LORD
ISLAND'S SHADOW LORD
IT'S MY ISLAND TOO!!
HE SAID "HIS ENTIRE KINGDOM," BUT IT'S ALL UNDERGROUND.
ADVENTURER
ORC
HE CAN JUST MAKE A COUNTRY THERE.
WITH US.
GRAH!
RAWR!
GRAH!
BEFORE THAT...
...CAN I HAVE A MINUTE?

DO YOU REMEMBER I SAID...
...IF I SETTLED THIS, I WANTED TO TREAT YOU ALL TO A MEAL?
I'D LIKE YOU TO KEEP THAT PROMISE FIRST!
AH...
WHAT PROMISE?
CAPTAIN MITHRUN AGREED TO IT.
WHILE YOU WERE AWAY.
OH...
WELL, THAT SHOULD BE FINE.
TELL US WHAT YOU WANT TO EAT.
I ALREADY HAVE THE INGREDIENTS.
NO!
IN SHORT ...

...I WANT YOU TO HELP US EAT MY LITTLE SISTER!
DON (BAM)

NOBODY MENTIONED THIS TO ME!!
ARE YOU STILL UNDER THE DEMON'S INFLUENCE !?
ARE YOU CRACKED!? DO YOU NEED YOUR HEAD EXAMINED !?
FOR RELIGIOUS REASONS, I CAN'T EAT MEAT...
EVEN THE IRRELIGIOUS DON'T WANT TO EAT HUMANS.
HE'S ALWAYS BEEN LIKE THIS, BUT EVEN SO, HE'S INSANE.
ENOUGH OF THIS!
I WON'T LET YOU DEFILE HER FURTH—
OH!
WE...

...HAVE BEEN EATING MONSTERS THIS WHOLE TIME.
WE FOUGHT THE RED DRAGON, THE LUNATIC MAGICIAN, AND THE WINGED LION...
...ALL IN ORDER TO RETAKE MY SISTER!
SHE'S BEEN FUSED WITH A DRAGON. TO GET HER BACK TO NORMAL...
...WE BELIEVE OUR BEST OPTION IS TO RESURRECT HER AFTER CONSUMING THE DRAGON PARTS.
Resurrect
Digest
EVERYTHING ELSE WAS SECONDARY.
HOW-EVER...
...IF WHAT WE DID MADE YOU HAPPY, OR IF YOU PITY HER AT ALL...
...A SINGLE BOWL OF SOUP IS FINE.
YOU CAN EVEN JUST HELP COOK...
...BUT WOULD YOU LEND US YOUR AID?
......
SHIN (SILENCE)

SIGH...
WELL, IT IS A LOT TO ASK.
WE'LL GET STARTED ON OUR OWN.
IF YOU FEEL LIKE IT, JOIN US WHENEVER YOU WANT.
COME ON. LET'S GO.
THAT SAID...
...HOW ARE WE GOING TO COOK THIS?

IT'LL TAKE MORE THAN US FIVE.
WHY DID YOU TELL THEM THAT?
I ASSUMED IF I PUT IT THAT WAY, SOMEONE WOULD HELP...
...BUT I GUESS NOBODY'S COMING.
THIS GUY...
FIRST, WHY DON'T WE BREAK THE ICE?
HOLD ON.
WE'RE FAR TOO SHORT ON UTENSILS.
WE'LL NEED TO COLLECT POTS FROM ALL OVER THE ISLAND.
WE NEED A BIG SPACE TOO!
THE ISLAND'S A WRECK RIGHT NOW.
WE MIGHT NEED TO GO TO KAHKA BRUD FOR POTS.
THE ICE WON'T LAST FOR-EVER...
WE NEED TO THINK OF A WAY TO PRESERVE FALIN.
I DON'T WANT HER TO ROT...
...AND THERE'S NO TELLING HOW LONG THE DUNGEON'S RULES WILL APPLY.
SO LONG AS WE YET LIVE, SHE SHOULD BE ALL RIGHT.

YAAD!
AND THE CITIZENS OF THE GOLDEN COUNTRY!
WE'LL HELP YOU.
THANKS.
ARE YOU FEELING ALL RIGHT?
...ACTU-ALLY...
IT FEELS AS IF A VEIL THAT COVERED US...
...IS GRADUALLY THINNING.
WE WEREN'T AWARE OF IT BEFORE...
WHEN THE VEIL VANISHES, IT'S POSSIBLE THAT WE'LL DIE.
...BUT IT MAY BE WHAT KEPT US FROM DEATH.
IT APPEARS WE STILL HAVE TIME, THOUGH!
LET US REPAY YOU WHILE WE CAN.
Y-YAAD...!

CLEAN THIS PLACE UP.
CLEAR OUT THE DEBRIS.
MM-HMM, MM-HMM.
DO YOU THINK WE COULD ASK THAT GUY FOR HELP TOO...?
WHAT GUY?
THE ELF WHO USES TELEPORTATION MAGIC.
THAT WOULD MAKE IT EASIER TO MOVE FALIN AND CUT HER UP.
Cut!
HUH...?
I MEAN, IT WOULD, BUT...
HE DIDN'T SEEM VERY REASONABLE...
WON'T THE ELVES ARREST YOU IF YOU GET TOO CLOSE RIGHT NOW?
MAYBE...
I DON'T THINK SO.
...

IF YOU'RE WORRIED, I'LL TRY TALKING TO THEM.
KABRU!
IF THEY WANTED TO CAPTURE YOU, THEY WOULD HAVE DONE SO ALREADY.
NO NEED TO LEAN ON THE ELVES.
I BET YOU COULD CUT HER UP REAL EASY WITH THAT SWORD.
ICE AND ALL.
I REFUSE TO LAY A HAND ON HER!!
OH, I SEE.
TCH.
SHURO! NA-MARI!
ALL THREE OF YOU CAME TO HELP!?
GYUUUU (HUG)
THAT'S GREAT!
IF THIS WILL SAVE HER, THEN I'LL COOPERATE.
YOU SWEAR YOU DON'T JUST WANT TO SEE HOW SHE TASTES!?
O-OF COURSE NOT.
WELL, THAT'S A RELIEF.
I BET THE REST WILL TRICKLE IN.
THE REST?

カラン
KARAN (CLANK)
カラン
KARAN
ぞろ
ZORO (TROMP)
カラン
KARAN
カラ
KARA
カラン
KARAN
ぞろ
ZORO
ぞろ
ZORO
THE ORCS.
OHO!
UTEN-SILS!
WE COLLECTED STUFF THAT WASHED UP FROM THE DUNGEON.
CAN YOU USE THESE?
OF COURSE, OF COURSE.
DO YOU NEED ANYTHING ELSE?
HMM.
SPICES AND INGRE-DIENTS WOULD BE—
ドサ
DOSA (WHUMP)
ドサ
DOSA
ドサ
DOSA

SIR DWARF!
IF YOU'D LIKE, YOU'RE WELCOME TO USE SOME OF OUR PROVISIONS.
OH, SORRY. MY BAD.
THOSE FLEW A LITTLE TOO FAR.
OH... OHO!
ALL THIS? ARE YOU SURE?
YES.
OUR QUEEN SAID TO AID YOU TO THE BEST OF OUR ABILITIES...
SHE'S ALREADY TRYING TO PUT HIM IN HER DEBT.
MM-HMM!
WHAT ELSE DO YOU NEED?
WELL, AS YOU'D EXPECT ...
MAN-POWER AND STOM-ACHS!
LEAVE THAT TO US, THEN.

MY TUMMY'S ALL GRUMBLY.
AT THIS POINT, I BET I COULD EAT AS MUCH AS THEY GIVE ME.
THE ADVENTURERS ...
...AND EVERYONE ELSE...
JUST HANG ON, FALIN...

IT WON'T BE LONG NOW...
...BEFORE WE EAT YOU!!
YOU MEAN "SAVE YOU"!!
YOU REALLY DO WANT TO SEE HOW SHE TASTES!

CHAPTER 93: THE END

94. Falin -2-

HEY, LAIOS!
WHERE DO YOU WANT THESE POTS?
OH, THOSE SHOULD GO...
HOLD IT, LAIOS!
THERE'S A LIMIT TO HOW MUCH WE CAN COOK OVER OPEN FIRES.
WE SHOULD TRY TO BORROW SOME PLACES IN TOWN.
TRUE.
IN THAT CASE, I'LL—
ぎゅるるるる〜…
GYURURU (GRUMBLE)
どっ
DO (GUFFAW)
THAT WAS LOUD.
—THE DEMON IS GONE.
THAT MAN ATE IT.
...YOUR MAJESTY...

HAVE THE HUMAN RACES BEEN SAVED...?
WILL MAGIC VANISH?
WHAT WILL BECOME OF THE WORLD?
......
THINGS ARE IN CHAOS OUT THERE AS WELL.
NO RESPONSE...
PERSON-ALLY, I THINK...
...THE DEMON WAS A PERSONALITY MANA DEVELOPED IN ORDER TO COMMUNICATE WITH HUMANS...
...AND THAT'S WHAT WAS DESTROYED.
IF THAT'S THE CASE, MANA AND MAGIC SHOULDN'T VANISH...
...BUT THERE'S NO WAY TO TELL HOW IT WILL AFFECT THE WORLD YET.
IT MIGHT GET A BIT HARDER TO MANAGE.

UM, EXCUSE ME.
GASA (RUSTLE)
GASA
I HAVE A REQUEST...
YES? WHAT IS IT?
WE'RE ABOUT TO START BUTCHERING AND COOKING THE DRAGON PARTS...
...AND WE'D LIKE HIS HELP.
HUH ...? CAPTAIN MITHRUN'S?
THE DRAGON IS MASSIVE.
PHYSICALLY MOVING AND CUTTING IT WILL BE REALLY DIFFICULT.
SO YOU'D LIKE TO USE TELEPORTA-TION...
I SEE.
HMM...
THAT MAY NOT BE POSSIBLE.
HUH?
IT WILL BE FASTER TO SHOW YOU.

CAPTAIN MITHRUN...
CAPTAIN. SHE'S CALLING YOU.
TSUN (POKE) TSUN
YUSA (SHAKE) YUSA
CAP-TAAAIN.
MUKYU (PINCH)
ARE YOU TRYING TO KILL HIM!?
BOKO (POW)
HE'S BASICALLY DEAD ALREADY.
HOW COULD YOU SAY THAT!?
WELL, COME OOON!

HE JUST DROPPED LIKE HIS STRINGS HAD BEEN CUT.
WE CAN PINCH HIM OR CAST SPELLS ON HIM, AND HE DOES NOTHING.
...YOU SEE?
THE DEMON ATE MOST OF HIS DESIRES.
ALL HE HAD LEFT WAS HIS DESIRE TO OVERTHROW THE DEMON. THAT WAS WHAT KEPT HIM GOING.
NOW THAT IT'S OVER, HE DOESN'T FEEL LIKE DOING ANYTHING.
I GUESS THERE'S ...
...NOTH-ING TO DO ABOUT THAT.
PROBABLY THE SAME.
WE'LL JUST START CHIPPING THE ICE AWAY BY HAND...
BUTSU (MUMBLE)
BUTSU
D—
DON'T GIVE ME THAT.

YOU PROMISED HIM, REMEMBER?
YOU NEED TO KEEP YOUR WORD!
NO DESIRES?
THAT'S AN ILLUSION.
YOU'RE JUST BURNED OUT, THAT'S ALL.
HEY.
QUIT ACTING LIKE YOU'RE PALS.
JUST 'COS YOU SPENT SOME TIME TOGETHER DOESN'T MEAN YOU KNOW HIM.
OH, WHY NOT?
KEEP GOING.
I WANT TO HEAR WHAT HE SAYS.

...MITHRUN.
EVEN IF YOU NEVER RECOVER WHAT THE DEMON ATE...
...I DON'T THINK YOU CAN EVER RUN OUT OF DESIRES.
FOR EXAMPLE, RIGHT NOW I'M THINKING...
"I WANT YOU TO LIVE A LIFE THAT'S NOT ABOUT REVENGE.
"I'D REALLY RATHER NOT EAT DRAGON MEAT IF IT WERE POSSIBLE...
HUH!?
"...BUT FOR THE SAKE OF MY FRIEND, I WANT TO HELP THEM FINISH IT."
A LITTLE WHILE AGO, I DIDN'T WANT ANY OF THAT.
PIKU (TWITCH)
EVEN IF YOU STUFF YOURSELF, YOU'LL BE HUNGRY AGAIN THE DAY AFTER.
HE MOVED.
AS LONG AS YOU'RE ALIVE, YOU'LL KEEP ACQUIRING NEW DESIRES.
LIKE IT OR NOT.

THA—
THAT'S RIGHT, CAPTAIN.
WHY NOT TAKE UP A NEW HOBBY?
SOMETHING YOU'VE NEVER TRIED BEFORE.
MAYBE HE COULD ...
...ADOPT A DOG, SAY?
OR LEARN A NEW LANGUAGE.
THIS ISN'T A MID-LIFE CRISIS, PEOPLE.
HE'S DONE MOST OF THAT STUFF.
HE'S A NOBLE.
MORONS.
THINK LOWER CLASS.
WHAT ABOUT MAKING NOODLES?
I HEAR THE HANDMADE STUFF IS REAL TASTY.
OR POTTERY?
YOU COULD SERVE FOOD YOU MADE IN A BOWL YOU MADE.
HEY, I LIKE IT!
LIKE MARCILLE'S...
WE WON'T BE EXPLORING DUNGEONS NOW ANYWAY!!
GO ENJOY YOUR SECOND LIFE.
WE'LL HELP, OKAY!?
NO, YOU'LL ALL BE GOING BACK TO PRISON...
OR... WELL...
IT WOULD BE NICE IF YOU WERE PARDONED...

I DOUBT YOU'LL FIND SOMETHING RIGHT AWAY...
...BUT EAT, REST UP A BIT...
...AND THEN START LOOKING FOR A NEW DESIRE.
OKAY?
CAP-TAIN...
CAP-TAIN!

...OKAY.
WHOA.

DOKI (BADMP)
ドキ
DOKI
ドキ
HARA (FRET)
ハラ
HARA
ハラ
BA (FWOOP)
バッ

PA (POOF)
AAH!
ZU (SLIDE)
ズ…
HM?
H-HEY! SHE'S GOING TO LAND HARD!!
WAAAAAAH!!
GURAAAA (TOPPLE)
ぐらあ
あああ…
THIS IS BAD!! CATCH HER!!

VERY NICE!
KEEP GOING. WE'LL CUT UP THE DRAGON JUST LIKE THAT.
EASY! EASY!
TAKE THE CARVED MEAT TO THE COOKING AREA AND GROUP IT BY PARTS.
OKAY.
THAT THIN MEAT SLICE LOOKS EASY TO USE.
WHAT DO WE DO WITH HER HUMAN HALF?
KEEP IT SOMEWHERE COOL UNTIL WE'VE EATEN THE DRAGON...?
WE HAVE SEVERAL ICE MAGIC CASTERS.
HAVE THEM KEEP THE ICE FROM MELTING.
YES'M.
LOOKS LIKE THIS WILL WORK!
Y-YEAH.
....

SUPA (SKASH)
スパ
SUPA
スパッ
PORO
ポロ
PORO (TUMBLE)
ポロ

CAPTAIN! YOU SHOULD TAKE A BREAK SOON.
SUPA (SKASH)
YOU'LL EXHAUST YOUR MAGIC AGAIN.
SUPA
SUPA
SUPA
CAPTAIN.
YOU'RE GOING TO COL-LAPSE.
SUPAPA
CAPTAIN!
GU (GRAB)
GYO (SHOCK)

WHA... WHAT'S WRONG?
WHEN THE DEMON SPIT ME OUT, I REALIZED...
...THAT MY REMAINING DESIRE WASN'T "REVENGE."
I THINK...
THE LAST BITE LEFT ON THE PLATE.
VEGETABLE SCRAPS ON A CUTTING BOARD.
THAT'S ME.
...I JUST WANTED IT TO FINISH ME OFF.

BUT...
WITH THE DEMON GONE, I REALIZED I'M ONLY LEFTOVERS NOW...
...AND EVERYTHING IS POINTLESS.
...EVEN SO...
...I MAY BE ABLE TO HELP SOMEONE ELSE BE COMPLETELY CONSUMED.

YEAH...
ACTUALLY, YOU ABSOLUTELY HAVE TO HELP!
YOU PROMISED, SO EAT AT LEAST ENOUGH FOR ONE.
...YES!
RIGHT! THAT'S RIGHT.
EVEN TRUE SCRAPS CAN BE COMPOSTED.
STEM ENDS SOAKED IN WATER MAY PUT OUT NEW GROWTH.
...AND USE THEM TO MAKE A FLAVORFUL BROTH.
YOU CAN SAVE ODD VEGETABLE BITS...
UH, 'SCUSE ME!
DID SOMEONE MENTION VEGETABLE SCRAPS?
AHEM!
......
HEH.
THERE ARE ALL SORTS OF USES FOR THEM, SO DON'T JUST THROW THEM AWAY.
SEE YOU.

HEH HEH
HEH!
HEH HEH HEH...
C-CAP-TAIN?
I SEE. SO EVEN VEGETABLE SCRAPS ARE USEFUL.
YES, ALL RIGHT ...
PHEW.
THAT'S...
...GOOD TO HEAR.

Chapter 94: The End

95. Falin -3-

THIS WASN'T THE AGREEMENT!!
YOU DEFEATED THE LUNATIC MAGICIAN!
YOU MUST INHERIT THE WHOLE OF THIS LAND AS MY GRANDFATHER WISHED!
YOU CAN SAY THAT, BUT...
...THE ISLAND ALREADY HAS LORDS AND RESIDENTS.
THOSE AREN'T A KING!
"THOSE."
I DON'T KNOW A THING ABOUT POLITICS.
I'LL TEACH YOU!
YOU'LL BE FINE!
WOULDN'T IT MAKE MORE SENSE IF YOU BECAME KING?
IT'S YOUR BLOODLINE.
YOU ARE THE ONLY ONE WITH A LEGITIMATE CLAIM.
I'VE NEVER SEEN MASTER YAAD SO LIVELY.
ZA (SHF)

"JUST WHEN THE DEMON WAS ABOUT TO DESTROY THE WORLD, ONE MAN APPEARED.
"TRANS-FORMING INTO AN ENORMOUS DRAGON, HE SWALLOWED THE DEMON WHOLE.
"IN RECOGNITION OF THIS GREAT FEAT, THE PEOPLE MADE HIM THEIR KING..."
SOUNDS GOOD TO ME.
IT'S A PERFECT HEROIC EPIC.
YOU EMBEL-LISHED QUITE A BIT.
A DRAGON?
IN THE END, THAT SORT OF THING IS IMPORTANT.
LISTEN.
EITHER WAY, THERE'LL BE FIGHTING OVER THE ISLAND.
THE LONG-LIVED RACES IN PARTICULAR MUST WANT INFORMATION ABOUT THE DEMON.
IF WE JUST HAND IT TO THEM, WE'LL LOSE OUT.
FOR THE SAKE OF HUMANITY'S FUTURE, YOU SHOULD ACCEPT.
YOU...
...CAN SAY THAT, BUT...
BA (FWIP)
AS HIS COMPANION, YOU SPEAK TO HIM AS WELL!!

HOKEEE (DAZE)
ほけー
COMPANION? WHAT, ME?
YES, YOU.
YOU'VE TRAVELED THIS FAR WITH HIM. YOU MUST HAVE AN OPINION ON THIS.
UH, NOT REALLY.
I WASN'T WITH HIM 'COS I WANTED TO BE.
IS THAT TRUE!?
THEN WHY DID YOU TRAVEL WITH HIM ALL THIS WAY!?
"WHY"...?
OH! WHERE ARE YOU...

BECAUSE IT WAS MY ONLY OPTION...
...IF I WANTED TO BE FREE.
OH RIGHT.
I DON'T HAVE TO STAY WITH THOSE GUYS NOW.
I'M FREE!
I CAN GO ANY-WHERE!
I DON'T HAVE TO EAT STUFF I DON'T LIKE!
FREEDOM
WHAT SHOULD I DO?

GASA (RUSTLE)
ガサ
GASA
ガサ
SENSHI.
WHAT ARE YOU GOING TO DO NOW?
HMM?
MAKE MEAT PIES.
I'LL GRIND THE LIVER AND BREAST MEAT TOGETHER, THEN BAKE THEM WITH PLENTY OF VEGETABLES AND SPICES.
FALIGON MEAT PIE
ENERGY
PROTEIN
FAT
CARBS
CALCIUM
IRON
VITAMIN A
VITAMIN B2
VITAMIN C
NO, I MEANT AFTER THIS...
WAIT!
ARE YOU PUTTING ALL THAT IN?
MAKE SOME WITHOUT VEGETABLES!
WHAT ARE YOU SAYING?

OUR INGREDIENT AND UTENSIL USE IS STRICTLY PLOTTED OUT.
I CAN'T JUST DO AS I PLEASE.
BUT I WANT TO EAT THAT PIE!
I CAN'T EAT IT IF IT'S GOT VEGETABLES IN IT.
YOUR DIGESTIVE SYSTEM ISN'T FELINE.
IF YOU WANT TO EAT THEM, THEN DO.
IF YOU DON'T WANT TO, YOU DON'T HAVE TO.
IZU-TSUMI... I'M WORRIED ABOUT YOU.
I WON'T BE ABLE TO LOOK AFTER YOU FOREVER.
AS A FREE SPIRIT, NO DOUBT YOU'LL CHOOSE ONLY WHAT YOU LIKE.
THAT'S FINE.
BUT REMEMBER THIS.
THAT NATURE OF YOURS MAY REDUCE YOUR FREEDOM AS WELL.
FROM NOW ON YOU MUST CHOOSE WHAT TO EAT AND WHAT TO AVOID.
ガブ
GABU (CHOMP)
I'LL EAT MEAT PIE WITH NO VEGETABLES, THEN!
GOT IT!?
HEY!
WHAT YOU'RE SAYING AND DOING DON'T MATCH—
ヒョイ
HYOI (YOINK)

SENSHI.
I BROUGHT LIVER.
THANK YOU.
CHOP IT FINELY TOGETHER WITH THOSE THINGS.
GOT IT.
BY THE WAY, SENSHI.
ARE YOU GOING TO LEAVE THIS PLACE?
TON (TMP)
YOU SAW WHAT THE DUNGEON'S LIKE.
I'LL LOOK FOR A PLACE WHERE I CAN BE SELF-SUFFICIENT.
THE ISLAND OR KAHKA BRUD WON'T DO?
THIS AREA SEEMS LIKE IT'LL BE NOISY FOR A WHILE.
TRAVELING WITH THEM WAS FUN...
...BUT IT DOESN'T NEED TO BE A CONSTANT FOR ME.
I'D LIKE TO ENJOY MY MEALS ALONE FOR A WHILE.
SURE, BUT SENSHI...

...A STRANGER WHO SHOWS UP OUT OF THE BLUE...
...ISN'T GOING TO BE ACCEPTED JUST ANYWHERE.
ORCS.
STRAY DWARVES.
BEAST-MEN.
WHO'S A WHAT!?
WHEREVER WE GO, NO ONE WANTS US.
SHOO!
SHOO!
THERE'S NO REFUGE FOR US.
YOU'VE LOST YOUR LANDS ENTIRELY. THIS WAS A TRAGEDY FOR YOU, WASN'T IT.
HMPH.
EVEN WITHOUT THIS, IT WOULDN'T HAVE LASTED FOREVER.
LOOK AT THAT.
クイ
KUI (NOD)
THE ISLANDERS AND THE ELVES ARE BEHAVING FOR NOW...
...BUT ONCE THE MEAL'S OVER, THEY'LL TRY TO EXPEL US.
WELL, WE CAN'T HAVE THAT.
THERE'S JUST ONE WAY TO SETTLE THIS PEACEFULLY.

LAIOS.
THE KING WHO RULED LONG BEFORE THE ISLAND'S LORD...
...NAMED LAIOS AS THE NEXT KING.
HE'S THE TRUE RULER.
ZAKU (SHUNK)
WILL THE IS-LANDERS ACCEPT HIM?
HOW NON-ISLANDERS REACT IS MORE IMPORTANT.
DWARVES AND ELVES ARE OLD-FASHIONED. THEY'LL RESPECT HISTORY.
IF THEY ACKNOWLEDGE HIM, THE LORD'S OPINION WON'T MATTER.
VERY GOOD!
VERY GOOD!
AND...

...IF MY SISTER BECOMES ONE OF HIS WIVES, WE'LL BE HIS PEOPLE.
IT WILL PLACE A HEAVY BURDEN ON YOU, THOUGH.
WHAT ARE YOU SAYING, BROTHER?
I'D BE HONORED TO SERVE AS OUR TRIBE'S FOUNDATION.
I'LL GLADLY... OFFER MYSELF TO...THAT MAN...
ポロリ
PORORI (TEARY)
...FOR-GIVE ME!
UU... UUUU!
I WONDER WHAT ORC SWEAT TASTES LIKE...
SHE REALLY DOESN'T WANT TO.
SO, SENSHI, PUT IN A WORD TO LAIOS FOR US.
I'M NOT REAL GOOD AT THAT.
GAH!
WHAT ARE THE OTHERS GOING TO DO?

DIGESTIVE ORGANS NEED TO BE CLEANED REALLY WELL, OR THINGS CAN GET UGLY.
IT'S A BIG JOB.
NO, I MEANT—
HUH? ME?
I'M MAKING SAUSAGE WITH THE BLOOD AND SMALL INTESTINE.
FALIGON BLOOD SAUSAGE
① ADD BLOOD TO FATTY MEAT, ORGANS, VEGETABLES, AND SPICES, THEN MIX.
② PACK THE MIXTURE INTO THE INTESTINE.
③ BOIL, AND IT'S DONE!!
ENERGY
PROTEIN
FAT
CARBS
CALCIUM
IRON
VITAMIN A
VITAMIN B2
VITAMIN C
YOU CAN'T EARN MONEY IN THE DUNGEON NOW.
NO, NOT THAT.
I MEAN AFTER WE EAT ALL THIS.
OH, THAT.
HUH...
THAT SOUNDS TASTY.

I WAS GOING TO RETIRE FROM ADVENTURING ANYWAY.
I'LL RUN A SHOP IN KAHKA BRUD.
I'VE ALREADY GOT A PLACE.
A SHOP?
A LOCK-SMITH.
THERE'S DEMAND FOR THOSE IN THE CITY.
IT MIGHT NOT HAPPEN FOR A BIT, THOUGH.
WHEN THE DUNGEON COLLAPSED, IT PUT A LOT OF HALF-FOOTS OUT OF WORK.
WASH THE INTESTINE WELL, CLEANING OUT DIRT AND EXCESS FAT.
I'LL BE RUNNING AROUND FOR THEM FOR A WHILE.
HUH?
WHY YOU?
EVERY-THING'S OVER. JUST DO WHAT YOU WANT.
LISTEN.
LOTS OF MY PEOPLE CAN'T PUT FOOD ON THE TABLE.
YOU THINK I COULD IGNORE THEM AND FEAST?
...WELL, I GUESS IT'S NOT YOUR PROBLEM.
JABU
ジャブ
JABU (SPLOSH)
ジャブ
IT'S FINE. THIS IS WHAT I WANT TO DO.
IRA (IRK)
イラ
イラ
IRA

BY THE WAY, HAVE YOU SEEN LAIOS?
YEAH.
THEY WERE BADGER-ING HIM TO BE KING.
AHH.
WHAT DO YOU THINK OF THAT?
I'M WONDERING WHY HE'S STILL HESITATING THIS LATE IN THE GAME.
I DO THINK HE COULD GIVE IT A TRY.
"KING" SOUNDS LIKE A BIG DEAL...
...BUT FORTU-NATELY THIS IS A TINY ISLAND.
HE PULLED THIS OFF, SO IT'LL WORK OUT SOMEHOW.
BESIDES, ANYBODY WOULD BE BETTER THAN THE LORD WE'VE GOT.
IT SOUNDS LIKE A PAIN.
HE WON'T GET TO DO WHAT HE LIKES ANY-MORE.
NAH, IT'S THE OTHER WAY AROUND.

WHAT WILL HE BE, NOW THAT HE'S NOT AN ADVENTURER?
A MERCENARY? A SAILOR?
HE'S NOT EDUCATED ENOUGH TO BE A SCHOLAR.
BUT HERE, HE COULD CALL IN RESEARCHERS AND HAVE THEM STUDY THE DUNGEON AND MONSTERS.
...MAYBE. I DUNNO.
STILL, HE'LL BE USEFUL.
YOU CAN'T HAVE EVERY LITTLE THING THE WAY YOU WANT IT.
......
BY THE WAY...
DID HE SEEM WEIRD AT ALL?
HE'S ALWAYS WEIRD.
WELL, YEAH, BUT...
...HE SEEMED DISTRACTED.
OR MAYBE THAT'S NORMAL UNDER THE CIRCUMSTANCES.

TO ISOLATE HER HUMAN HALF...
...WE NEED TO EAT EVERY LAST BIT OF THE DRAGON.
......
I'M GOING TO USE THE SHIN AND TAIL MEAT IN A STEW.
ME?
FALIGON STEW
① CUT UP TAIL MEAT AND VEGETABLES, THEN STEW.
② KEEP STEWING.
③ DONE!
ENERGY
PROTEIN
FAT
CARBS
CALCIUM
IRON
VITAMIN A
VITAMIN B2
VITAMIN C
SHE'LL BE COMING WITH US.
ACTUALLY, WE WERE JUST TALKING ABOUT IT...
I'M ASKING ABOUT YOUR FUTURE.
OH, THAT!?

THERE'S NO POINT IN HIDING ANCIENT MAGIC WHEN THE DEMON'S GONE...
...BUT RULES ARE RULES...
...AND THE ISLAND'S LORD AGREED TO GIVE US ANYONE WHO USED IT.
I'M VERY SORRY, BUT...
Use of ancient magic
SO...
...YOU'RE GETTING ARRESTED?
NH...
ARE THEY GOING TO WHIP YOU AND PILE WEIGHTS ON YOUR KNEES AND STUFF?
MAYBE THEY'LL RIP HER FINGER-NAILS OFF!
WE'LL DO NO SUCH THING!
SHE'LL JUST LIVE IN CUSTODY FOR A WHILE.
HOW LONG IS "A WHILE"?
I REALLY COULDN'T SAY...
IT'S FINE!
I KNEW WHAT I WAS DOING!
I WOULD HAVE REGRETTED NOT DOING IT MORE!
ONLY...
UM...
IF MY SEN-TENCE IS A LONG ONE...
...I MAY NOT SEE ANY OF YOU FOR QUITE SOME TIME...

...WELL. IT'LL BE A LITTLE LONELY...
...BUT IF WE CAN WRITE TO EACH OTHER, IT MIGHT BE OKAY...
IN LIGHT OF YOUR ACHIEVEMENTS, I'M SURE THEY'LL BE A BIT LENIENT.
WHY'S SHE GOING EASY ON HER?
THANKS ...
WHAT DOES SHE MEAN, "THANKS" ?
IRA (IRK) イラ
IRA イラ
IRA イラ
AND YOU, IZU-TSUMI?
WHAT ARE YOU GOING TO DO?
I'M GONNA...
...DO WHAT I WANT.
I SEE. GOOD.
THAT'S THE BEST WAY.
OH! BUT...
...YOU MUSTN'T BE TOO PICKY.
DON'T JUST EAT WHAT YOU LIKE.
GRR...
EAT SOME VEGGIES TOO.
IF YOU DON'T...

...YOU WON'T LIVE A LONG TIME...
...SO WE'LL NEVER SEE EACH OTHER AGAIN.
NH!
...I MEAN, IF YOU LIVE BY YOUR-SELF...
...YOU'LL JUST EAT SNACKS AND MEAT EVERY DAY...
...AND SLEEP WHEN-EVER YOU WANT...
...AND YOU'LL NEVER EXERCISE...
THERE'S JUST NO WAY YOU'LL LIVE A LONG LIFE!!
NOBODY ASKED YOU TO CARE!
TRY REALLY HARD AND LIVE 700 YEARS!!
I CAN'T!!
WAAAAH!

RRGH, THAT TICKS ME OFF.
WHY AM I SO ANNOYED?
I'M FINALLY FREE.
I CAN HAVE EVERYTHING THE WAY I WANT IT...
...SO WHY—
BECAUSE I CAN'T HAVE EVERYTHING THE WAY I WANT IT.
SENSHI WON'T COOK FOR ME.
CHILCHUCK'S GOING OFF SOMEWHERE FOR SOMEBODY ELSE.
MARCILLE WILL BE EATING PRISON FOOD ABROAD.
YAAD'S ALL DES-PERATE TO MAKE LAIOS KING.
I WON'T GET TO SEE WHOEVER I WANT WHEN I WANT TO.
IF I ONLY EAT WHAT I LIKE, I'LL TRASH MY HEALTH.
JUST DOING WHAT I WANT WON'T KEEP ME FED IN THE FIRST PLACE.

WAIT. IF THE WINGED LION HAD EATEN ME, COULD I HAVE...?
HM?
I CAN'T HAVE EVERYTHING THE WAY I WANT IT IF I'M GONNA LIVE.
HOW UNFAIR IS THAT?
YAAAH!
I NEED TO PICK THE STUFF I REALLY WANT TO DO.
WHAT DO I MOST WANT TO DO, RIGHT NOW?
YEAH. THAT.

BOOO (DAAAZE)
ぼー
FOUND HIM.
GASA (RUSTLE)
ガサ
LAIOS.
WHAT ARE YOU GOING TO DO NOW?
ドキリ
DOKIRI (BADMP)
HUH!?
I... I'M...
I MEANT COOKING.
GAKU (SLUMP)
ガク
I WAS THINKING ABOUT THE BONES AND HIDE.
HUMANS CAN'T REALLY CONSUME EVERY LAST BIT.
WE'LL EXTRACT ALL THE BROTH WE CAN, THEN CRUSH THE BONES, COOK THEM...
...AND SCATTER THEM IN THE WOODS.
HOPEFULLY THE PLANTS WILL EAT SOME OF THEM THAT WAY.

IF I MAKE THEM DO ALL THIS...
...AND THEN THE RESURRECTION DOESN'T WORK...
...I BET THEY'LL ALL BE DISAPPOINTED.
HUH?
THEY'LL HAVE EATEN THINGS THEY DIDN'T WANT TO EAT...
...AND ALL FOR NOTHING.
WILL THEY THINK I TRICKED THEM?
HAAAAAH!
LISTEN... DON'T YOU KNOW?
EVERYBODY HAS TO EAT STUFF THEY DON'T WANT TO EAT SOMETIMES...
HMPH!

THAT MEANS IT'S FINE IF THEY DON'T GET TO EAT WHAT THEY WANT NOW AND THEN.
THEY'LL CHOOSE WHETHER TO EAT OR NOT.
WHAT'S REALLY ANNOYING IS WHEN YOU DON'T EVEN GET A CHOICE.
PEOPLE WITH NOWHERE TO LIVE.
PEOPLE WITH NOTHING TO EAT.
PEOPLE WHO CAN'T SEE OTHERS WHEN THEY WANT TO.
WHAT ARE YOU GOING TO DO NOW?
I'LL...

I WANT TO THANK THE PEOPLE WHO HELPED WITH FALIN'S RESURRECTION.
I'D LIKE TO MAKE A PLACE...
...WHERE THEY CAN EAT WHAT THEY WANT...
...WITH PEOPLE THEY LIKE.
EVEN IF THE RESUR-RECTION DOESN'T WORK...
...I WANT TO THANK EVERYONE WHO WAS INVOLVED.
TO THAT END, I'LL DO WHAT I CAN.
HMM.

TRUE.
I'LL HAVE TO TAKE RESPON-SIBILITY.
AH!
I MEAN, TO BEGIN WITH, EVERYBODY ONLY HAS IT ROUGH BECAUSE YOU ATE THE WINGED LION.
MOST OF MANKIND ALREADY HATES YOU FOR THAT.
PHEW...
WHAT ARE YOU GOING TO DO, IZUTSUMI?
I AL-READY MADE UP MY MIND.
I'M GONNA EAT THE MEAT PIE SENSHI'S MAKING.
IT'S DONE!!!

Chapter 95: The End

96. Falin -4-

YAAD...
WHAT IS THIS?
ARE THEY STILL MAD THAT WE BROKE THEM UP WITH HOLY WATER?
NO, NO.
THEY'RE HAPPY.
THEY'VE BEEN DISEMBODIED FOR AGES, SO THEIR MINDS HAD GONE HAZY...
...BUT THE AIR OF THE SURFACE...
...AND A NEW KING HAVE PERKED THEM RIGHT UP.
THEY'RE PROPOSING IDEAS FOR YOUR CORONATION CEREMONY.
C-CORONATION CEREMONY?

I SEE.
SO THIS DINNER PARTY IS THE BEST OPPORTUNITY TO ANNOUNCE MY KINGSHIP?
THAT'S RIGHT!
GASA (RUSTLE)
THE WESTERN ELVES AND OFFICIALS FROM KAHKA BRUD ARE HERE AS WELL.
I'D LIKE TO GIVE HIM A BIT MORE DIGNITY.
YES, THE DWARVES WON'T TAKE YOU SERIOUSLY IF YOU'RE BEARDLESS.
IF ONLY WE HAD MY GRAND-FATHER'S CLOTHING AND ACCOUTRE-MENTS...
SADLY, THEY ALL SANK...
WANT US TO GUSSY HIM UP?
THAT'S NOT QUITE WHAT WE'RE AFTER...
IF THEY UNDERESTI-MATE YOU, YOU'RE FINISHED.
PLAT-FORM SHOES.
WHY NOT PUT A LITTLE CHARCOAL AROUND HIS EYES?
MAYBE JUST SHAVE IT ALL...
HE'S JUST SO DRAB.
BEARD.
IF YOU WANT ME TO BE KING...
...THEN LET ME HANDLE THIS.

WATCH IT, COMING THROUGH.
FALIGON GRATIN
ENERGY
PROTEIN
FAT
CARBS
CALCIUM
IRON
VITAMIN A
VITAMIN B2
VITAMIN C
MAKE WAY FOR THE GRATIN.
HEY, MARCILLE!
GRATIN'S READY.
OOH!
THAT LOOKS SOOO GOOD.
IT SMELLS GREAT.
YEAH, IF YOU DON'T KNOW WHAT'S IN IT.
PUT IT ON THE TABLE OVER THERE, OKAY?
SURE THING.
UM. EXCUSE ME.
WHAT ABOUT THIS DISH?
THAT GOES OVER THERE!
AND THIS SOUP!?
IT GOES HERE!
WAA WAA WAA (CLAMOR)
WE'RE NOT DONE.
THE KITCHEN'S TURNING 'EM OUT FAST.
SOME OF THE DISHES WILL TAKE TIME...

THIS IS SHAPING UP TO BE A BANQUET THAT WILL LAST FOR DAYS!
WE HAD TO JURY-RIG A VENUE, BUT IT LOOKS PRETTY GOOD.
LET'S DIG IN ALREADY.
WHERE IS THE HOST?
HE WAS TALKING WITH YAAD OVER THERE...
ZAWA (MURMUR)
ZAWA
ZAWA
WHAT, WHAT?
WHAT HAP-PENED!?
OH...

HEY, DEMON-EATER!
THREE-HEADED LAIOS.
MONSTER-EATER!
BOSO (MUMBLE)
...VEGGIE ARMOR.
DRAGON-SLAYER!
LORD OF THE DUN-GEON!
PERVY TALL-MAN.
DEMON KING LAIOS!

KING LAIOS, DEVOURER OF THE BIZARRE!
RAAAAH!
アアアアア

IS THIS FROM THAT ONE CAR-CASS?
THAT'S YOU ALL OVER.
I MEAN, IT'S FINE, BUT...
DO YOU NEED THAT?
...IT WAS PROBABLY THE LAND'S GUARDIAN BEAST UNTIL THE DEMON TOOK ITS PLACE.
AND I DON'T THINK THE WINGED LION'S DESIRE TO MAKE PEOPLE HAPPY WAS A LIE.
I DON'T WANT TO ERASE HIM.
I WANT HIM TO KEEP WATCHING OVER US.
CHIRA (PEEK)
BE-SIDES...
...THE ORCS WEAR BITS OF WHAT THEY'VE EATEN AS MEMENTOS TOO.
IT'S REALLY COOL...
THESE ARE TRO-PHIES!!
THEY'RE NOT A RECORD OF OUR MEALS!

GO ON, STEP UP.
SAY A FEW WORDS TO THEM.
DISPLAY YOUR POWER TO THE PEOPLE.
YEAH, GIVE 'EM SOMETHING THAT'LL GO DOWN IN LEGEND AND SONG.
DON'T YOU DARE TALK ABOUT YOUR HOBBIES.
JUST RELAX AND SPEAK FROM THE HEART.
WORDS THAT WILL MAKE PEOPLE HAPPY...
RAAAH!

WAAH!
HE GOT US.
THE ISLAND'S HIS NOW.
WHAT? NO! IT CAN'T BE...
AAAH!
GOOD GRIEF.
CAN YOU HEAR THIS, YOUR MAJESTY?
WHAT SHOULD WE DO?
RAH...
...IT WOULD BE A SHAME TO BORE YOU AND LET THE FOOD GET COLD.
GU (RAISE)
UH...
I THOUGHT OF A FEW THINGS I COULD SAY, BUT...

LET'S GET STARTED!
EVERYONE, PLEASE EAT YOUR FILL.
RAH!

IF THERE'S AN UNKNOWN TOXIN IN THIS MEAT...
!
...THIS TALE REALLY WILL GO DOWN IN HISTORY.
MOUNTAINS OF CORPSES
IT'LL BE A GREAT LESSON ON THE DANGERS OF FOOD POISONING, FOR SURE.
PAKUN (MUNCH)
ぱくん
YUM!
IT IS GOOD, ISN'T IT?
...I SWEAR.
MOGU (CHEW)
モグ
MY REPORT TO KAHKA BRUD IS GOING TO BE A LENGTHY ONE.
HOWAA (SPARKLE)
ほわあ
THE MEAT MELTS IN YOUR MOUTH, AND IT GOES SO WELL WITH THE SAUCE AND THE RICE...
IT'S COMPLETELY DELISH!!
...SO SHE SAYS, YOUNG MASTER.
I SEE...

YOUNG MASTER.
YOU NEEDN'T FORCE YOURSELF.
I COULDN'T PROTECT HER...
...AND I COULDN'T FULLY BELIEVE IN LAIOS.
HOKA
HOKA (STEAM)
THIS IS MY SIN.
KA (SCARF)
I HUMBLY PARTAKE!
LOOK AT YOU WOLF THAT DOWN, YOUNG MASTER!
YOU WON'T BEAT ME, THOUGH!
WHAT MAN EATS A RICE BOWL WITH A FACE LIKE THAT?
MM.
THIS IS GOOD...
NO DOUBT THIS FINE FLAVOR...
...WILL MAKE FOR A FINE TRAVEL STORY.
......
YES, YOUNG MASTER.

DO YOU THINK A BIT OF THE DUNGEON'S MYSTERIES WILL BE REVEALED TO THE WORLD NOW?
THEY'D SURE BETTER.
THAT'S WHY WE DID WHAT WE DID.
EVERYONE CHOSE RIGHT.
IF EVEN ONE THING HAD BEEN MISSING...
...WE WOULDN'T HAVE GOTTEN HERE.
WAS THIS REALLY RIGHT?
WE WON'T SUDDENLY END UP WITH A KINGDOM OF MONSTERS, WILL WE!?
I DUNNO!
NEVER MIND, JUST EAT, ALREADY!
HAAH...
...I THOUGHT IF THE DUNGEON DISAPPEARED, IT WOULD SOLVE EVERYTHING...
...BUT I BET WE'LL SPEND OUR WHOLE LIVES WORRYING.
HEH..
THAT'S WHAT HUMANS DO...
HURRY UP AND EAT!!

AAAAAH!
I-IT'S DELICIOUS...!
IT'S MILDER THAN I FIGURED IT WOULD BE.
I COULD PROBABLY TAKE THIS FOR BEEF OR PORK.
I COULDN'T PROCESS IT PROPERLY, SO I WAS CONCERNED...
...BUT IT'S MORE TENDER THAN THE RED DRAGON WE ATE BEFORE, AND QUITE EASY TO COOK.
TRUE...
FOR A MONSTER, THE TEXTURE MIGHT BE THE EQUIVALENT OF A NEWBORN CHICK.
OOH, THIS IS GOOD.
YOU'RE SO TASTY, FALIN...
QUIT IT.
WHAT WE'RE EATING IS THE RED DRAGON.
IT'S NOT FALIN.
THERE'S NO TELLING WHAT HER TAKE ON IT IS, THOUGH.

NEVER MIND THAT, YOU'RE EATING YOUR HAIR TOO.
OH! YOU'RE RIGHT.
....
IT'S IN THE WAY. TIE IT BACK LIKE YOU USUALLY DO.
......
THE THING IS...
ゴクン
GOKUN (SWALLOW)
...I LOST THE DESIRE TO TAKE CARE OF MY HAIR...
...AND I SORT OF FORGOT HOW TO TIE IT BACK.
DID THE WINGED LION EAT IT?
OH.
YEAH. ...MAYBE?
THAT'S ...
I BET IT WAS VERY TASTY.
GIMME YOUR HAIR TIES.
I'LL DO IT.

WHA—? THAT'S AMAZING!
THANK YOU, CHILCHUCK.
I DID RAISE THREE DAUGHTERS, YOU KNOW.
CHILCHUCK, COME TO THE WEST WITH ME AND DO MY HAIR EVERY DAY!
NOT EVEN FUNNY!
I CAN'T BELIEVE I DID THIS EVERY DAY.
WHAT'LL I DO NOW?
AHH, NOW IT'S EASIER TO EAT.
THAT STYLE MIGHT BE A LITTLE YOUNG FOR HER.
MAR-CILLE...
ABOUT THAT...
I GUESS I'LL JUST HAVE TO CHOP IT ALL OFF.

WOULD YOU STAY ON THE ISLAND?
......?
I'LL BE SPENDING MY DAYS DIGGING UP THE DUNGEON FOR A WHILE.
THE LONG-LIVED RACES KNOW ABOUT MAGIC AND MONSTERS...
...BUT TO MOST OF THE SHORT-LIVED RACES THEY'RE FRIGHTENING, MYSTERIOUS THINGS.
FALIN ISN'T THE ONLY ONE WHO WAS RUN OUT OF HER HOMETOWN.
ANCIENT CIVILIZATIONS, THE UTILITY OF MAGIC...
...HOW TO USE MONSTERS AND MINIMIZE DAMAGE FROM THEM...
I WANT TO COMMUNICATE ALL OF THAT.
I'D LIKE TO MONETIZE IT TOO, OF COURSE, BUT...
...ANYWAY. IT WOULD REALLY HELP TO HAVE SOMEONE WHO KNOWS ABOUT MAGIC HERE.
CHIRA (PEEK)
ちら

THAT SOUNDS GREAT!
I'D LOVE TO HELP!
...I HAVE TO GO TO THE WEST.
I'LL REFER A FRIEND TO YOU INSTEAD.
BUT...
REALLY?
!
NO.
COME WITH ME A SEC, OKAY?
WHERE ARE WE GOING?

NGH...
OH, HELLO.
THE FOOD IS DELICIOUS. THANK YOU.
DID YOU NEED SOME-THING?
IT'S NOTHING IMPORTANT.
FEEL FREE TO KEEP EATING.
I INTEND TO KEEP MARCILLE UNDER OBSERVATION HERE.
...YOU WHAT?
I DEFEATED THE LUNATIC MAGICIAN, AND SO THIS ENTIRE LAND IS MINE.
THE ISLAND LORD PROMISED TO GIVE YOU ANYONE WHO'D USED ANCIENT MAGIC...
...BUT HE'S NOT ME.
I DON'T AGREE.
GATA (CLATTER)
YOU'RE QUIB-BLING—

IF YOU DISCLOSE ALL THESE THINGS AND I'M CONVINCED, I'LL CONSIDER IT.
HOW DOES IT RELATE TO THE DUNGEON AND THE DEMON?
HOW GREAT A THREAT IS IT?
WHAT IS ANCIENT MAGIC?
WHY IS SIMPLY USING OR KNOWING IT A CRIME?
WAIT A—
Enough, Patta-dol.
The rest isn't a job for your group.
LET'S GO, MARCILLE.
SORRY TO IN-TERRUPT YOU.
THANK YOU FOR DONATING INGREDI-ENTS.
I HOPE YOU'LL STAY A WHILE AND EAT ALL YOU CAN.

YOUR MAJESTY.
Is the meat good?
YEAH, IT'S NOT BAD, MA'AM.
I'm glad to hear it.
I ate something similar long ago, and it was awful.
SOMETHING SIMILAR?
THAT LAND, THE DEMON'S FATE, AND THAT LITTLE GIRL WILL ALL NEED WATCHING...
...BUT "THE SPELL THAT GRANTS ANY WISH" HAS BEEN LOST.
THERE IS TIME.
Rest your wings for a while.
By the way—
Does the role of diplomat interest you?
WHAT?

WAIT, WAIT.
CHAKA (HUSTLE)
チャカ
CHAKA
チャカ
CHAKA
チャカ
LET'S GET SOME DISTANCE, FAST.
WHY THE RUSH?
PEOPLE THINK I DEFEATED THE LUNATIC MAGICIAN, BUT I TOTALLY DIDN'T.
SOSOKUSA (SCUTTLE)
そそくさ
WE'LL HAVE TROUBLE IF THEY FIND OUT.
IT'LL BE FINE.
NO ONE ELSE WAS THERE TO SEE IT.
SISSEL'S STILL ALIVE.
HE MIGHT WAKE UP.
IF HE DOES, I'LL BE HAPPY.
HE SAVED ME.
WANT TO GO CHECK ON HIM?

BIKURI (STARTLE)
YAAD...
LAIOS.
WHAT ARE YOU DOING THERE?
HOW'S SISSEL?
THERE'S BEEN NO CHANGE.
HE WON'T EAT OR DRINK...
...SO I FEAR HE MAY STARVE.
THAT...
GUUU (GRUMBLE)
THAT'S REALLY ROUGH!
IF WE PUT IT IN HIS MOUTH, HE MAY SWAL-LOW.
WOULD YOU HOLD HIM UP?
BE CAREFUL HE DOESN'T CHOKE.
HERE! SMELLS GREAT, DOESN'T IT!?
AH!

IT'S THE NEW KING!
YOUR MAJESTY!
COME AND EAT WITH US.
YOUR MAJESTYYY.
OH... NO, I'M...
YOUR MAJESTY!
YOUR MAJESTY!
GO ON, YOUR MAJESTY!
PIKURI (TWITCH)
ピクリ
SISSEL?
......
THIS WAY, OVER HERE!
COME ON! COME EAT, COME DRINK.
LIFE'S ABOUT TO GET ROUGH, SO YOU'D BETTER EAT LOTS.

I NEVER THOUGHT I'D TASTE ANYTHING AGAIN...
...BUT FOOD'S REAL GOOD WHEN YOU CAN SEE THE SKY, HUH.
COME ON, KING LAIOS, DRINK UP.

YOU GO, YOUR MAJESTY!
LOOK AT YOU PUT THAT AWAY!
YOUR...
...MAJ-ESTY...
SISSEL!?
YOU'RE AWAKE!?
HOW ABOUT SOME WATER?
ARE YOU HUNGRY?
DELGAL.
HUH!?
OH... YES!
IT'S ME!! MM-HMM!!

OH GOOD...
YOU WERE OUT LATE. I WAS WORRIED.
I SEE YOU MADE IT IN TIME FOR DINNER.
I'M SORRY, SISSEL!
I SHOULDN'T HAVE LEFT WITHOUT TELLING YOU.
IT'S ALL RIGHT NOW, THOUGH.
WANT SOME SOUP?
IT'S VERY TASTY.
I DON'T NEED IT.
I DON'T NEED ANYTHING ANYMORE.
SISSEL...

LISTEN.
LONG AGO, I WAS AFRAID OF DYING AND LOSING EVERY-THING...
...BUT NOW IT DOESN'T SCARE ME THAT MUCH.
EVEN AS WE SPEAK ...
...ALL SORTS OF CREATURES ARE EATING OR BEING EATEN...
...AND CIRCULATING THROUGH VARIOUS PLACES.
WE'RE JUST A PART OF THE CYCLE...
...SO I'M NOT THAT FRIGHTENED ANYMORE.
I'M SORRY I MADE SUCH A SELFISH REQUEST.
PLEASE DON'T WORRY ANYMORE, SISSEL.
SO IT'S ALL RIGHT...
...

THIS TERRITORY'S PURE TROUBLE.
THE LONG-LIVED RACES HAVE BEEN STEALING IT FROM EACH OTHER FOR AGES.
THE FIGHTING NEVER STOPPED.
WHEN THEY PUT THE SHORT-LIVED RACES IN CHARGE OF IT, THINGS FINALLY SETTLED DOWN...
...BUT THEY BOTH WATCH AND MEDDLE.
CROPS ARE OFTEN POOR.
GOVERNING THE PLACE IS BOUND TO BE A HEADACHE.
THINGS ARE GOING TO GET ROUGH...
...KING LAIOS!
AHEM.
IT'S A REALLY SMALL ISLAND, THOUGH.
I WON'T EXPECT MUCH, AND WE'LL GET BY.
MY FATHER'S A VILLAGE CHIEF, SO... I KNOW A BIT ABOUT THIS SORT OF THING.
A VILLAGE CHIEF?
SMALL ISLAND?
WHAT ARE YOU TALKING ABOUT?

ゴッ
GO (RUMBLE)
ガタ
GATA
AGH! THE FOOD!
ガチャ
GATA (CLATTER)
ガタ
GATA
AN EARTH-QUAKE?
ズゴゴゴゴゴ
ZUGO (RUMBLE)
GO
GO
GO
GO
VOLCANO?
WHAT HAP-PENED?
わぁ
WAA (CLAMOR)
わぁ
WAA
OUT THERE.
LOOK OFFSHORE.

THE GOLDEN COUNTRY USED TO BE A CONTINENT !?
THE—
INDEED, IT DID.
SISSEL'S MAGIC CAME UNDONE...
...AND THE KINGDOM SWALLOWED BY THE EARTH IS RETURNING TO ITS FORMER STATE.
YOU KNOW, THE KAHKA BRUD COASTLINE DOES HAVE A FUNNY SHAPE...
KAHKA BRUD
ISLAND
SO IT'S WHAT REMAINED AFTER THIS AREA VANISHED?
KAHKA BRUD
MERINI?
MOUN-TAIN?
BFFT!
WELL, HEY.
AT LEAST NOW YOU WON'T HAVE TO DIG IT UP.
DWAH HA
HA
THEY DO SAY A BIG PLATE CAN SERVE AS A SMALL ONE.
HA!
HEH.
TRUE ...
HA
IT LOOKS LIKE IT'S GOING TO BE A FUN COUNTRY.
HA
HA
HA!
CHAPTER 96: THE END

FINAL CHAPTER: DELICIOUS IN DUNGEON

"ONE MAN HAS RETAKEN THE FALLEN ANCIENT LAND FROM THE DEMON'S THROAT!"
RUMOR SAYS IT'S MADE WITH HUMAN FLESH AND MONSTERS.
BUT EVERY-BODY SAID IT WAS GOOD!
THE RUMOR CROSSED THE SEA, ECHOING FAR AND WIDE.
FREE FOOD?
THEY SAY IF WE BRING VEGETABLES, THEY'LL FEED US MEAT.
ISN'T THE NEXT DISH DONE YET?
SIT TIGHT JUST A BIT LONGER.
THE FRIED STUFF'S SOLD OUT.
LINE UP.

THE FEAST WENT ON FOR SEVEN DAYS AND NIGHTS.
MEANWHILE, BIT BY BIT THE GOLDEN CASTLE SURFACED...
...SLOWLY REGAINING ITS FORMER SHAPE.

FALIGON CREAM STEW
ENERGY
PROTEIN
FAT
CARBS
CALCIUM
IRON
VITAMIN A
VITAMIN B2
VITAMIN C
THE CREAM STEW...
BABAAAN (KA-DOOOM)
...IS DONE!!
CREAM STEW.
SORRY. I'M STUFFED.
IT'S DONE.
I'VE JUST EATEN.
CREAM STEW.
WE CAN'T EAT ANY MORE!
I SUP-POSE...
...HAVING THE SAME MEAT FOR A WEEK WOULD GROW MONOTO-NOUS.
FOR ALL BUT A FEW, THAT IS...

THE CREAM STEW IS DONE!!
ばーん
BAAAN (BOOM)
FORCING YOURSELF ISN'T GOOD.
WELL ...
KA カッ
KA (SCARF)
KA
...WE'VE ALMOST FINISHED IT, RIGHT?
ARE YOU FULL ALREADY?
I CAN'T. I'M DONE.
I'LL EAT IT!! WAIT A SECOND!!
WE HAVE TO HANG IN THERE.
ヒョイ
HYOI (LIFT)

HOW MUCH MORE IS THERE REALLY?
TONS, I BET.
I SAW IT TWO DAYS AGO, AND WE'D BARELY MADE A DENT.
PAKU PAKU (CHOMP)
MORI (NOM) MORI
ACTU-ALLY...
URP!
...THERE'S NOT MUCH TO GO!
THAT POT'S THE LAST OF IT.
HUH!?
EVEN THOUGH WE HAD SO MUCH LEFT!?
OVER THE PAST FEW DAYS, WE SUDDENLY GOT MORE VISITORS.
IT DWINDLED AWAY BEFORE OUR EYES.
THEN... WHAT ARE THEY EATING NOW!?
YUM.
THIS'S GOOD STUFF.
NORMAL FOOD THEY BROUGHT IN.
I THOUGHT YOU'D WANT TO EAT THE FINAL DISH...
...SO I KEPT BACK THE LAST OF THE MEAT.

ZUKOO (SLUMP)
WHAT THE HECK !!?
OH, PHEW! SERI-OUSLY...
I WAS SCARED WE WEREN'T GETTING THROUGH IT!!
HAAH...
YOU DID SEEM TO BE BROODING.
WELL, EVERYBODY LOOKED LIKE THEY WERE GETTING TIRED OF EATING!
I THOUGHT WE HAD TO FINISH THIS OUR-SELVES ...!!
HAAAH...
THAT'S A RELIEF, THOUGH.
LAIOS, IT'S OKAY. YOU DON'T HAVE TO PUSH...
...YOUR-SELF...
GOKU (GULP)
GOKU
GOKU
PERORI (LICK)
THANKS FOR THE FOOD!
NO WAY!! YOU ATE IT ALL!?
HUH!?
I'M SORRY...
IT WAS GOOD, SO I JUST...
THAT'S FINE, BUT AREN'T YOU OVER-EATING!?
DIDN'T YOU JUST EAT ANOTHER POT OF SOMETHING ELSE?
UM.
I'M NOT FULL YET, THOUGH.

HAS YOUR APPETITE GONE WEIRD...
...BECAUSE YOU ATE THE DEMON'S APPETITE?
W-WEIRD?
HAVE YOU ACQUIRED AN INFINITE APPETITE?
TH-THAT COULD BE!
ACTU-ALLY—
IS IT THE DEMON'S POWER!?
Devil's Stomach
Human Body
KEEP THAT UP, AND YOU'LL PACK ON WEIGHT LIKE CRAZY.
YOUR BODY'S STILL HUMAN.
HE'LL NEED TO PRACTICE STRICT PORTION CONTROL FROM NOW ON, OR ELSE.
OBESITY CA CAUSE LIFESTY DISEASES AND MANY OTHER ILLNESSES IF
WAIT...
THEN YOU MEAN I'LL SPEND THE REST OF MY LIFE...
...FEELING A LITTLE HUNGRY?
I IMAGINE SO.
POOR GUY.
N-NO...

DOES IT HURT?
NO.
IT'LL FEEL LIKE I'M ALWAYS LESS THAN HALF FULL, THOUGH.
I'D LIKE TO EAT JUST A BIT MORE.
SENSHI, CAN I HAVE—
AS I SAID, THIS POT WAS THE LAST OF IT.
OH. I SEE...
HUH?
YOU MEAN...
WE...
WE FINISHED IT OFF.

HOORAY!
ANY LEFT-OVERS ANY-WHERE!?
NONE!
WE ACTUALLY RAN SHORT, SO WE'VE STARTED SERVING REGULAR FOOD.
WHAT ABOUT THE BONES, HIDE, AND FAT!?
CRUSHED AND SCAT-TERED IN THE FOREST AND THE OCEAN!
WE'LL LET THE PLANTS AND MICROBES HANDLE THE REST.
*PLEASE DON'T DO THIS.
AND FALIN'S UPPER HALF?
READY TO GO!
WE'VE LEFT A BIT OF THE DRAGON ...
...TO USE IN RECON-STRUCTING HER LEGS...
...BUT IN TERMS OF REMAINING SOUL, FALIN SHOULD WIN BY A MILE.
THEN SHE'LL USE HER OWN POWERS OF RECOVERY...
...AND REVIVE IN HUMAN FORM!

...HEY.
SPIT IT OUT. WHY ARE YOU SO DE-PRESSED?
I-I'M NOT DEPRESSED OR ANYTH—
LIAR!! IT'S OBVIOUS!!
YOU'RE HIDING SOME-THING, AREN'T YOU!?
GASU (THWOK)
HURRY UP!
SPILL!
BOKO
YOU!
BOKO (BONK)
WHAT A PAIN IN THE BUTT...
FINE. I'LL TALK.
THE THING IS...
...I THINK...
...FALIN'S RESURRECTION MIGHT NOT SUCCEED.

THE WINGED LION SAID...
I CURSE YOU.
YOUR GREATEST WISH WILL NEVER COME TRUE NOW.
AND THAT WAS FALIN'S RESURREC-TION?
THAT'S RIGHT.
I CAN'T BE TOTALLY SURE...
...BUT I DON'T THINK MY GREATEST WISH...
...COULD BE ANYTHING ELSE.
......
C'MERE A SEC...
FIRST OFF...

FRANKLY, I DOUBT SOMETHING ADMIRABLE LIKE...
I WANT TO RESURRECT MY SISTER!
...COULD EVER BE THAT GUY'S GREATEST WISH.
AGREED.
I'M NOT SAYING HE DOESN'T LOVE HER.
YEAH, THERE'S JUST NO WAY.
NO COMMENT.
I BET HIS WISH IS TO BE A MONSTER.
THAT WOULD EXPLAIN WHY HE CHANGED BACK.
AYE.
OH! BUT...
...WHATEVER YOU DO, DON'T SAY THAT TO HIM.
WHY NOT?
IT WOULD HURT HIM.
AHEM!
LAIOS!
LISTEN...
THAT ISN'T NEWS TO US.
WE KNOW SUCCESS ISN'T GUARANTEED.

THIS IS GOING TO SOUND STRANGE...
...BUT I THINK THIS JOURNEY...
...WAS MEANT TO HELP US ACCEPT DEATH.
SINCE THE DUNGEON LET US REVIVE, WE ALMOST FORGOT...
...BUT LIVES ARE FUELED BY OTHER LIVES.
WE'RE NO EXCEPTION.
I COULDN'T ACCEPT THAT, AND I PITCHED A FIT.
BUT ...
...AS I WAS SEPARATING FALIN'S FLESH AND BONE...
...AND COOKING IT...

SO...
...EVEN IF HER RES-URRECTION FAILS...
...IT'S OKAY.
I CAN ACCEPT IT THIS TIME.
IT WON'T BE THE DEMON'S FAULT EITHER.

GAAAAH!
DON'T TALK AS IF YOU KNOW.
NOT WHEN YOU'RE ONLY A FEW DECADES OLD.
THERE WAS A TIME WHEN I FELT ENLIGHTENED LIKE THAT TOO.
ZORO (TROMP)
ZORO
ZORO
ABOUT A CENTURY AGO.
WHAT NEXT? "BE GRATEFUL TO ALL LIFE"?
GRATITUDE WON'T MAKE THE CREATURES YOU'VE EATEN HAPPY.
LIFE AND DEATH DON'T MEAN MUCH.
THAT GNOME IS SPITEFUL.
SO?
WILL YOU TRY TO REVIVE HER OR NOT?
WE—
WE WILL.
YOU'D BETTER, AFTER YOU MADE US EAT THAT ATROCITY!!
WE'LL HELP AS WELL.
WE CAN'T HAVE YOU MAKING ANOTHER CHIMERA.
THANK YOU...
IF THE GIRL INTENDS TO LIVE, NO DOUBT SHE WILL.

TO BE HONEST, THIS RESURRECTION WILL BE DIFFICULT.
HER LOWER BODY AND DIGESTIVE ORGANS WILL NEED TO BE RECON-STRUCTED.
WELL, SPECIALISTS WILL HANDLE THE HARD PARTS.
WE'RE READY TO GO.
WE NEED YOU TO STIMULATE HER MEMORIES OF BEING HUMAN.
TALK TO HER AND GIVE HER MANA.
FALIN.

くん
KUN (SNIFF)
SOME-THING SMELLS GOOD.
THIS WAY...
OVER HERE...
I CAN'T GO. MY LEGS ARE—
HUH?
WHEN DID IT GET THIS SMALL?
IN THAT CASE, I MIGHT BE ABLE TO MANAGE.
ずり
ZURI (DRAG)

HFF!
HFF!
コロン
KORON (ROLL)
ジタ
JITA (FLAIL)
バタ
BATA (KICK)

GO ON. EAT.
DAAA (DROOL)
だー
MUGU (NOMF)
むぐ
CHEW IT WELL.
YOUR DIGESTIVE SYSTEM ISN'T FULLY RECOVERED YET.
MOGU (CHEW)
モグ
モグ
MOGU
GOKURI (GULP)
SWALLOW IT.

CAN YOU TELL?
IT GOES DOWN YOUR ESOPHAGUS...
...TO YOUR STOMACH.
FROM SMALL INTESTINE TO LARGE.
IT'S USED AND ABSORBED THROUGH EVERY INCH OF YOU.
IT TRAVELS ALL THROUGH YOUR BODY...
...AND GIVES YOU SHAPE.

IS IT GOOD?
YES, VERY.
WOULD YOU LIKE MORE?
YES!

WELL.
I SUPPOSE IT'S NOTHING TO DO WITH ME.
HMM.
GO.
THAT PATH IS OBVIOUSLY HARDER AND CRUELER, BUT...

ZZZ...
ZZZ...
SNRR...
NNN...
ガス
GASU (WHUNK)
NGH!

FALIN.
HUH?
WHA ...?
REALLY?
HUH?
IS THIS THE WINGED LION'S TRAP?
NO... BUT...

THANK GOODNESS!!

DON'T TELL ME I WAY OVERSLEPT AGAIN.
YOU DID.
YOU JUST WEREN'T WAKING UP, SO WE WERE SCARED IT HAD FAILED.
YOU WON'T SAY "KIDDING!" AND FALL APART, RIGHT?
OR TURN INTO A DRAGON AGAIN?
FA—
FALIN!!!
GYUUUU (GLOMP)
OH, GOOD! I'M SO GLAD...!
YES, WE ALL ARE.
DOES ANYTHING FEEL WEIRD?
LIKE, UM... YOUR LEGS, SAY.
MY LEGS?
BASA (RUSTLE)

SORRY. WE ATE AS MUCH AS WE COULD, BUT...
THERE WAS NO WAY TO GET ALL OF IT...
...THIS IS EXCEL-LENT.
OH, HON-ESTLY!
ぎゅ
GYUUUUUU (HUUUUUUG)
YOU DUMMY!
HEY, QUIT. ARE YOU TRYING TO SUFFOCATE HER AGAIN?

CHIL-CHUCK!
AND...
SENSHI!
YOU RE-MEMBER HIM?
HE COOKED FOR US, RIGHT?
I MADE THE CURRY TOO.
AND THIS IS IZU-TSUMI.
SHE'S HELPED US WITH LOTS OF THINGS—
AND SHE'S SHY.
ARE WE... OUT OF THE DUN-GEON?
THAT'S RIGHT.
OH.
YOU SHOULDN'T GET UP YET—

GACHA (KACHAK)
ガチャー
AGH!
DOKI DOKI (BADMP)
ドキドキ
FOR NOW, COME GET DRESSED.
RELAX AND TAKE YOUR TIME.
I'LL GET A MEAL READY.

YOU CAN DISCUSS WHAT HAPPENED...
...AND WHAT YOU SHOULD DO NEXT...
...AT YOUR LEISURE, WHILE YOU EAT.

THEY'RE
ALL GOOD
PEOPLE.

I'M NOT SURE WHY, BUT THEY GAVE ME THINGS.
EVERYONE'S BEEN WANTING TO MEET YOU.
THEY SAID IT'S WINE FROM THE GOLDEN CASTLE.
WHOOPS!
NOT TODAY. SAVE IT FOR LATER.
HAVE SOMETHING THAT'S EASY ON YOUR DIGESTION.
EGG AND CARROT MUSH
ENERGY
PROTEIN
FAT
CARBS
CALCIUM
IRON
VITAMIN A
VITAMIN B2
VITAMIN C
ONCE YOU'RE BACK IN SHAPE, I'LL GET YOU WHATEVER YOU WANT.
WHAT DO YOU WANT TO EAT?
I HAD PIZZA LAST TIME...
WELL, UM...
LIVING ARMOR FIRST, OF COURSE.
HUH!?
YOU'RE STARTING WITH THAT!?
AND SO...

THE KINGDOM WHICH HAD FALLEN A MILLENNIUM AGO RESURFACED.
WITH AWE AND REVERENCE, THE PEOPLE CALLED THEIR NEW TALL-MAN KING "DEVOURER OF THE BIZARRE."
NATURALLY, BUILDING A NATION ON LAND RECLAIMED FROM THE SEA...
...WAS NO EASY TASK.
EVEN WITH BRILLIANT FOLLOWERS, THE KING SUFFERED GRIEVOUS HARDSHIP.
IN ADDITION, VICIOUS BANDITS WERE A FREQUENT MENACE.
HOWEVER, THE MONSTERS WHO HAD APPEARED WITH THE CASTLE...
...WERE A WARD AGAINST TRUE CRISES.

FOR SOME REASON, THE MONSTERS DREADED THE KING AND NEVER CAME NEAR HIM...
...AND SO HIS CITIZENS' LIVES WERE PEACEFUL.
ACCORDING TO LEGEND, THE KING SAID...
SO THIS WAS THE "CURSE," HUH?
...AND WAS DISCONSOLATE, BUT THAT MAY NOT BE TRUE.
FOOD PRODUCTION AND PRESERVATION INTERESTED THE KING...
...AND HE SPENT HIS LIFE AVIDLY RESEARCHING TECHNIQUES THAT USED MAGIC AND MONSTERS.
WHILE MANY FAILED...
...A FEW EXPERIMENTS SUCCEEDED, AND THE POOR BOTH WITHIN AND WITHOUT HIS BORDERS WERE FED.
WHEN THE CHILDREN FROM TOWN ASKED HIM...
"WHY DO YOU CARE ABOUT FOOD SO MUCH?"
...THE KING RESPONDED...

EATING IS THE EXCLUSIVE PRIVILEGE OF THE LIVING.
IN ORDER TO LIVE, WE HAVE TO KEEP EATING.
NOW THEN, IT'S MEALTIME.
WHAT SHOULD WE HAVE TODAY?

FINAL CHAPTER: THE END

KENSUKE

MISC. MONSTER TALES 14

AAAAH...
I'M BEAT.
ALL I DO IS TALK TO PEOPLE EVERY DAY.
I GET ENOUGH SLEEP, I HAVE FREE TIME...
...BUT IT'S MORE TIRING THAN EXPLORING THE DUNGEON.
YOU'RE JUST NOT USED TO IT.
IT'S BEEN A YEAR. I DON'T THINK I'LL EVER GET USED TO IT.
KABRU WOULD BE MUCH BETTER AT THIS.
HE'S GOT THE ENERGY FOR IT TOO.
DON'T SAY THAT.
HE'S DOING A LOT TO HELP YOU, LAIOS.
I HAVE NO REGRETS...
...BUT I MISS THE DUNGEON SOME-TIMES.
I WANT TO SEE LIVE MONSTERS, NOT THE CORPSES IZUTSUMI BRINGS ME.
PAY ME FIRST.
THEN LET'S GO TO A DUNGEON.

FALIN!
THERE ARE A FEW NATURAL DUNGEONS NEAR THE CASTLE.
WANT TO VISIT ONE?
WHAT ARE YOU SAYING!?
BUT IF I GET CLOSE, THE MONSTERS RUN AWAY.
THAT'S GOOD.
STRONG MANA TENDS TO POOL IN THIS AREA.
IF WE LEAVE THE NATURAL DUNGEONS ALONE, DANGEROUS MONSTERS MIGHT MOVE IN.
THAT MEANS ...
I SHOULD GO RUN THEM OFF?
THAT...
HAS THIS SHRUNK A BIT?
NO, YOU'VE PUT ON WEIGHT.
WHY NOT USE ANOTHER SUIT?
GYU (TIGHT)
IF I DON'T USE THIS ONCE IN A WHILE, IT'LL RUST.
KENSUKE TOO.
ZAN (TA-DAA)
...SOUNDS LIKE MY CUE!!
AW, GEEEEZ!
YOU GOT HIM ALL WORKED UP!!

AAAGH. ARE YOU SURE?
SNEAKING OUT LIKE THIS...
IT CAN'T BE OKAY.
WHAT IF SOMETHING HAPPENS?
MONSTERS ARE ONE THING, BUT WHAT IF WE RUN INTO BANDITS? OR BEARS?
IT'LL BE FINE.
HE HAS THE TWO OF US.
HERE WE ARE!
THIS HOLE IS PRETTY DEEP. THEY WERE WORKING TO SEAL IT OFF...
...BUT SEVERAL PEOPLE SAW A BIG MONSTER, SO THE WORK'S BEEN SUSPENDED.
WELL, LET'S GO HAVE A LOOK.
IT'S QUIET.
I BET THEY'VE ALL RUN AWAY.
THE DUNG AND TRACKS ARE STILL FRESH.
JUST AT A GLANCE ...
...I'D SAY WALKING MUSHROOMS, SLIMES, BIG BATS...
ON THEIR OWN, THEY AREN'T MUCH OF A THREAT...
...BUT WE DON'T WANT THE MONSTERS THAT EAT THEM SETTLING HERE.
LET'S GO IN A BIT FARTHER.

IT DOES LOOK AS IF SOME-THING'S HERE.
SOME-THING PRETTY BIG.
WHAT DO YOU THINK IT IS?
A SOLITARY OMNIVORE.
DRAKE, SHAPE-SHIFTER, GRIFFIN...
HMM...
NOT THIS, NOT THAT...
WHAT ABOUT KEN-SUKE?
IF IT SENSED A RISKY MONSTER, WOULDN'T IT ALERT US?
ACTU-ALLY...
...KENSUKE HAS BEEN DEAD FOR QUITE A WHILE.
HUH!?
I BET HE'S ALL DRIED OUT IN THERE.
HE SEEMED WEAK TO ENVIRONMENTAL CHANGES, AND THEN I TOOK HIM ALL OVER THE PLACE.
BRR!
GLUB!
GLUB!
PLUS, THE WINGED LION TOOK CONTROL OF HIM. HE HAD AN AWFUL TIME.
WAH!
AH!
HE DOESN'T EAT, AND HE DOESN'T RUN FROM ME...
...SO THAT'S HOW IT IS.
I SEE...
THAT'S TOO BAD.

I'M SORRY YOU NEVER GOT TO EAT LIVING ARMOR.
IT'S FINE.
SENSHI FEEDS ME ALL SORTS OF MONSTERS.
NIYARI (SMIRK)
HUH... WHEN?
I RUN INTO HIM IN NATURAL DUNGEONS SOMETIMES.
LUCKY.
I WANT TO SEE SENSHI TOO.
CHILCHUCK AND THE ORCS MEET HIM A LOT...
...BUT HE DOESN'T COME TO THE CASTLE MUCH.
I JUST PASSED HIM.
HUH !?
I SAW HIM YESTERDAY.
HUH !?
I MISS BOTH HIM AND THE DUNGEON.
I MISS HIM SO MUCH THAT RANDOM ROCKS ARE STARTING TO LOOK LIKE HIM.
PFFT!
WHAT!?
I MEAN, THIS ONE'S THE SPITTING IMAGE OF—
IT REALLY LOOKS LIKE HIM, DOESN'T IT.
IT DOES. NATURE IS INCREDIBLE.

UWAAH!
BRAAWK!
ボコ
BOKO (THWOK)
LAIOS! ARE YOU OKAY!?
BOKO ボコ
BOKO ボコ
BOKO ボコ
I SEE. A COCKA-TRICE...!
SO THIS DUNGEON'S BIG MONSTER WAS A COCK-ATRICE?
I COMPLETELY DIDN'T SEE IT...
......
DID YOU KNOW SENSHI WAS HERE?
ZON'S PEOPLE SAID THEY HADN'T SEEN HIM IN A WHILE.
FROM THE CLUES, I THOUGHT HE MIGHT BE HERE.
WHY DIDN'T YOU TELL US!?
I WASN'T TRYING TO HIDE IT...
I SWEAR, YOU AND YOUR BROTHER!

SENSHI! IT'S BEEN AGES.
APOLOGIES FOR THE TROUBLE.
WE'RE GLAD YOU'RE OKAY.
I WASN'T EXPECTING TO SEE A COCKATRICE HERE.
I FOUGHT BACK, BUT IT BIT ME.
SO ITS INJURIES MEANT IT COULDN'T RUN FROM ME.
AHA...
WE CAN'T HAVE COCKATRICES THIS CLOSE TO A TOWN.
GO MAKE SURE THERE AREN'T ANY MORE.
WE'LL WAIT HERE.
OK~
LAI—
AUGH! SOMETHING JUST RAN UNDER MY FEET!
MARCILLE, BEHIND YOU!
WHAT, WHAT!? WHAT'S THERE!?
OH! IT WENT THAT WAY!
AGH! WHAT!? NOOO!
ボン!
BON (BOOMF)

GRILLED COCKATRICE
SKIN
WHITE MEAT
WITH LEEKS
IT'S DONE!!
WHAT'S WRONG, LAIOS?
YOU LOOK GLUM.
FOOD TASTES ESPECIALLY GOOD AFTER HARD WORK, HUH?
IT REALLY DOES.
IF IT HAD BEEN A DIFFERENT MONSTER, SENSHI WOULD HAVE BEEN DEAD.
...THEN I REALIZED I WOULD HAVE BEEN TOO.
...I WAS GLAD IT WAS A COCKATRICE AT FIRST.
ARE YOU RATTLED BECAUSE YOU DIDN'T NOTICE THE COCKA-TRICE?
THAT TOO, BUT...
IF THIS ADVENTURE SHOWED YOU THAT, THEN IT WAS WELL WORTH IT.
COMING HERE MIGHT HAVE BEEN...
...A LITTLE CARELESS.

I KNOW.
COULD WE LEAVE SOMETHING THAT SMELLS LIKE YOU?
THAT SHOULD REPEL THE MONSTERS FOR A WHILE.
THEN WE CAN START SEALING IT AGAIN.
OH, I SEE.
WHAT COULD WE USE?
HAIR OR URINE WOULDN'T WORK FOR LONG.
AT LEAST WE WON'T HAVE TO WORRY ABOUT HIM GETTING CHOPPED INTO BITS AND SOLD PIECEMEAL AROUND THE WORLD.
...OKAY.
I'LL LEAVE MY ARMOR AND KENSUKE.
YOU'RE SURE?
I'D FEEL BAD MAKING HIM STAY NEAR ME FOREVER.
BESIDES, IT'S QUIETER HERE.
IF THE ARMOR'S WITH HIM, HE'LL REST BETTER.
NAMARI'S GIVEN ME LOTS OF BATTLE GEAR.
THANK YOU, KENSUKE.
REST IN PEACE...

REMEMBER YOU ARE A KING, AND AS SUC
HE'S DOING GREAT. NOWHERE NEAR DUST YET.
...SHALL WE HEAD BACK AND ENDURE YAAD'S LECTURE TOGETHER?
ALL RIGHT. WELL...
LATER...
...THE DUNGEON'S MANA REVIVED KENSUKE, WHO HAD ONLY SEEMED DEAD.
MUSHA MUSHA (MUNCH)
FEEDING ON LAIOS'S ARMOR, HE WAS ABLE TO REPRODUCE ASEXUALLY.
A CENTURY LATER, RUMORS WOULD SURFACE REGARDING "THE GHOST OF THE KING...
"...WHO WANDERS IN SEARCH OF MONSTER FLESH"...
I'LL SEND NAMARI AND SHURO COCKATRICE FEATHERS.
I'VE GOT A BAD FEELING ABOUT THIS.
...BUT OUR PARTY COULD NOT HAVE KNOWN THAT.
DUN-GEON FOOD.
THERE'S NO HIERARCHY INVOLVED.
EATING IS, QUITE SIMPLY, THE EXCLUSIVE PRIVILEGE OF THE LIVING.
AH, DUNGEON FOOD.

Please do not remove living creatures from or introduce them to any environment.

ACKNOWLEDGMENTS

Thank you for helping me for such a long time, Wataru Ota-san, Ikeda-san, Itou-san, Suga-san, Taguchi-san, and all of my other assistants.

My supervising editor, who's supported the series since it began. The designer, who put so much work into the covers.

My family, who watched over me.

Most of all, I was able to keep drawing this series because of everyone who found and read it.

Truly, thank you so much.

14

DELICIOUS IN DUNGEON

RYOKO KUI

Translation: Taylor Engel Lettering: Abigail Blackman

This book is a work of fiction. Names, characters, places, and incidents are the product of the author's imagination or are used fictitiously. Any resemblance to actual events, locales, or persons, living or dead, is coincidental.

DUNGEON MESHI Volume 14 ©Ryoko Kui 2023
First published in Japan in 2023 by KADOKAWA CORPORATION, Tokyo. English translation rights arranged with KADOKAWA CORPORATION, Tokyo through TUTTLE-MORI AGENCY, INC., Tokyo.

English translation © 2024 by Yen Press, LLC

Yen Press, LLC supports the right to free expression and the value of copyright. The purpose of copyright is to encourage writers and artists to produce the creative works that enrich our culture.

The scanning, uploading, and distribution of this book without permission is a theft of the author's intellectual property. If you would like permission to use material from the book (other than for review purposes), please contact the publisher. Thank you for your support of the author's rights.

Yen Press
150 West 30th Street, 19th Floor
New York, NY 10001

Visit us at yenpress.com
facebook.com/yenpress
twitter.com/yenpress
yenpress.tumblr.com
instagram.com/yenpress

First Yen Press Edition: July 2024
Edited by Abigail Blackman & Yen Press Editorial: Thomas McAlister
Designed by Yen Press Design: Andy Swist

Yen Press is an imprint of Yen Press, LLC.
The Yen Press name and logo are trademarks of Yen Press, LLC.

The publisher is not responsible for websites (or their content) that are not owned by the publisher.

Library of Congress Control Number: 2017932141

ISBNs: 979-8-8554-0035-9 (paperback)
979-8-8554-0036-6 (ebook)

10 9 8 7 6 5 4 3 2

TPA

Printed in South Korea